THE FINAL FRONTIER
SCOTLAND'S EARLY ROMAN LANDSCAPE

ANDREW TIBBS

To my husband, Paul

Front cover: Castle Greg Fortlet.

Back cover: The site of the camp at Normandykes.

First published 2024

Amberley Publishing
The Hill, Stroud,
Gloucestershire, GL5 4EP

www.amberley-books.com

Copyright © Andrew Tibbs, 2024

The right of Andrew Tibbs to be identified as the Author
of this work has been asserted in accordance with the
Copyright, Designs and Patents Act 1988.

All rights reserved. No part of this book may be reprinted
or reproduced or utilised in any form or by any electronic,
mechanical or other means, now known or hereafter invented,
including photocopying and recording, or in any information
storage or retrieval system, without the permission in writing
from the Publishers.

ISBN: 978 1 3981 1723 5 (print)
ISBN: 978 1 3981 1724 2 (ebook)

British Library Cataloguing in Publication Data.
A catalogue record for this book is available from the British Library.

Typeset in 11pt on 14.5pt Celeste.
Typesetting by SJmagic DESIGN SERVICES, India.
Printed in the UK.

Appointed GPSR EU Representative: Easy Access System Europe Oü, 16879218
Address: Mustamäe tee 50, 10621, Tallinn, Estonia
Contact Details: gpsr.requests@easproject.com, +358 40 500 3575

Contents

	Acknowledgements	4
	Introduction	5
1	Scotland in the First Century	9
2	Fortification Types	12
3	Roman Fortress Scotland	18
4	Roman Control of Scottish Landscapes	23
5	The Early Fortifications	26
	Bibliography	85
	Index of Roman Sites	95

Acknowledgements

Many people have provided support and advice while undertaking the research that forms the basis of this book. My thanks to Professor Richard Hingley, Dr Rob Witcher, Dr David Petts, Dr Rob Collins, Professor David Breeze, Dr Rebecca Jones, the late Professor C. Sebastian Sommer, Erik Graafstal, Dr David Woolliscroft, Dr Birgitta Hoffmann, Martha Stewart and Janet Davies, widow of the late Roy Davies. I would also like to thank the following organisations who have supported the costs of undertaking this research: the Tameia Trust, the Gibson Graham Charitable Trust, the Robert Kiln Charitable Trust, Hatfield College, and the Hatfield College Trust. Finally, I would like to thank my husband, Dr Paul Bennett, whose support and advice has been both invaluable and unwavering.

Editorial Notes

All the images within this book are copyright the author, unless otherwise stated. The maps and any LiDAR images have been compiled and processed, where relevant, by the author and contain OS data ©Crown copyright and OS Terrain 5, OS Terrain 50, OS OpenMap – Local and Strategi right (2020, 2021, 2022). Some site data, particularly grid references and classifications, have been extracted from Canmore, the National Record of the Historic Environment in Scotland. Binary viewsheds (visibility analysis) has been calculated from an observer height of 10 metres for towers, and 8.6 metres from the fortress, camps, forts and fortlets with an observed height of 0 metres/ground level. The fort plans and some camp outlines have been drawn from various sources, including excavation reports, aerial photography and LiDAR imaging by the author. The remaining camp outlines have been adapted from previous research undertaken by Dr Rebecca Jones, for which I am grateful.

Introduction

The earliest Roman invasion of Scotland happened under the command of Julius Gnaeus Agricola, the Governor of Britain, sometime around AD 77–86/90. Agricola campaigned across Scotland, with Roman writers telling us he personally founded all the forts which were built at this time. This seems like a bit of a Roman exaggeration, given that the Imperial army had dedicated soldiers whose job it was to find the best locations for forts, clear the land, and plan out the fortification ahead of the rest of the army, who would then arrive and begin building. The Romans were expert engineers and considered a range of factors when choosing where to build their fortifications; they thought about how a site could be defended using the natural topography, where the river network was, which direction it would face, and where the local tribes were living.

Recent developments in modern digital technology, such as drones, laser scanning, and specialist computer software, have helped archaeologists to better understand Scotland in the Roman period. One technique, spatial analysis, brings together archaeological and mapping data in a specialised computer database. It helps archaeologists to identify new sites of interest and can indicate the role and function of Roman fortifications in the landscape, including why they were built in certain locations, and how they made use of the natural features of the landscape to protect themselves. This type of analysis has led archaeologists studying other parts of the Roman Empire to conclude that fortifications were usually built in places that allowed the army to control the landscape surrounding the military sites. Scotland is no different, with most of the early fortifications located in positions that allow the army to control movement through the landscape and those living within it. The suggestion that the Romans may have built forts in locations to enable them to control the native population was first suggested by John Abercromby in the early twentieth century. He noted that a series of Roman

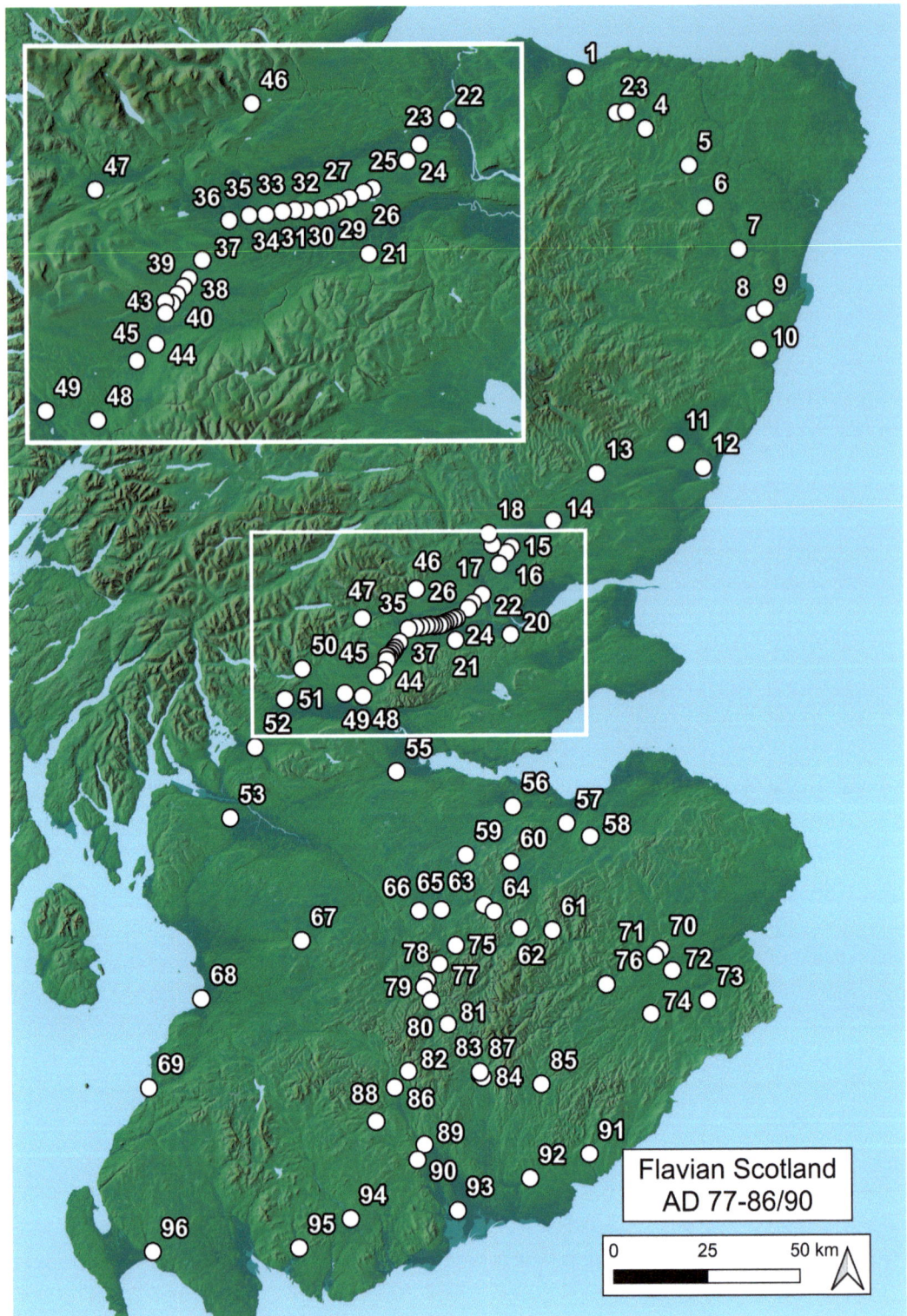

First-century Roman sites in Scotland.

Key

1. Bellie (Camp)
2. Auchinhove (Camp)
3. Muiryfold (Camp)
4. Burnfield (Camp)
5. Glenmailen (Ythan Wells) (Camps)
6. Logie Durno (Camp)
7. Kintore (Camp)
8. Normandykes (Camp)
9. Milltimber (Camp)
10. Raedykes (Camp)
11. Stracathro (Fort, Camp)
12. Dun (Camp)
13. Inverquharity (Camp, Fortlet)
14. Cardean (Fort)
15. Black Hill (Tower)
16. Cargill (Fort, Fortlet)
17. Inchtuthil (Fortress, Camps)
18. Gourdie, Steeds Stalls (Camp)
19. Woodhead (Tower)
20. Abernethy (Carey) (Camp)
21. Dunning (Camp)
22. Bertha (Fort)
23. West Mains of Huntingtower (Tower)
24. Peel (Tower)
25. Westmuir (Tower)
26. Thorny Hill (Tower)
27. Moss Side (Tower)
28. Witch Knowe (Tower)
29. Gask House (Tower)
30. Muir O' Fauld (Tower)
31. Kirkhill (Tower)
32. Roundlaw (Tower)
33. Ardunie (Tower)
34. Raith (Tower)
35. Parkneuk (Tower)
36. Strageath (Fort)
37. Westerton (Tower)
38. Kaims Castle (Fortlet)
39. Shielhill North (Tower)
40. Shielhill South (Tower)
41. Black Hill (Tower)
42. Ardoch II and V (Camps)
43. Ardoch (Fort)
44. Woodlea (Greenloaning) (Tower)
45. Glenbank (Fortlet)
46. Fendoch (Fort)
47. Dalginross (Fort, Camp)
48. Hillside, Dunblane (Camps)
49. Doune (Fort)
50. Bochastle (Fort, Camp)
51. Malling (Fort, Camps)
52. Drumquhassle (Fort)
53. Barochan Hill (Fort)
54. Lochlands (Camps)
55. Camelon (Forts)
56. Gogar Green (Camp)
57. Elginhaugh (Fort)
58. Woodhead (Camp)
59. Castle Greg (Fortlet)
60. Carlops Spittal (Camp)
61. Eshiels (Camp)
62. Easter Happrew (Fort)
63. Kirkhouse (Camp)
64. Castlecraig (Camp)
65. Bankhead (Camp, Fortlet)
66. Castledykes (Fort, Camps)
67. Loudoun Hill (Fort)
68. Ayr (Camp)
69. Girvan Mains (Camps)
70. Newstead (Fort, Camps)
71. Eildon Hill North (Tower)
72. Hiltonshill (Camp)
73. Cappuck (Fort)
74. Denholm (Eastcote) (Camp)
75. Cornhill (Camp)
76. Oakwood (Fort, Camp)
77. Lamington (Camp)
78. Wandel (Camp)
79. Cold Chapel (Camp)
80. Crawford (Fort)
81. Beattock Summit (Tower)
82. Durisdeer (Camp)
83. Beattock: Barnhill (Fortlet), Bankend (Camp)
84. Milton (Fort, Camp)
85. Raeburnfoot (Camp)
86. Drumlanrig (Fort), Islafoot (Camp)
87. Beattock, Barnhill (Fortlet)
88. Kirkland (Fortlet)
89. Dalswinton: Bankhead (Fort), Bankfoot (Fort, Camps)
90. Fourmerkland (Camp)
91. Broomholm (Fort)
92. Birrens (Fort, Camp)
93. Ward Law (Fort)
94. Glenlochar (Fort, Camp)
95. Gatehouse of Fleet (Fortlet)
96. Glenluce (Camp)

forts located on the edge of the Scottish Highlands were positioned at the entrance to different valleys (known as glens). These glens were often the main routes into the Highlands, and so he theorised that the forts, which he called 'glen-blockers', were deliberately placed at the glen entrance to control the movement of the tribes.

We need to be careful when examining and drawing conclusions about Roman sites in Scotland because more often than not we know very little about individual sites – archaeologists rarely excavate a whole Roman fort or camp, and instead tend to investigate small areas within these. This makes it difficult to build up a profile of the whole site, and can often lead to assumptions being made which cannot really be proven one way or the other. When thinking about the earliest Roman sites in Scotland, there are several things we need to keep in mind: a small number of fortifications have shown some possible signs of being occupied before Agricola invaded; and after the Romans abandoned Scotland, towards the end of the first century, some sites were reoccupied and rebuilt as part of the later invasions. This can affect how we understand these sites. Archaeological or scientific evidence which helps archaeologists to date when the fortifications were built, abandoned and reoccupied is, for many sites, limited (and often based on theories); some sites have been badly affected by post-Roman development or by natural processes (such as erosion) affecting our ability to understand or interpret Roman activity at these.

This book is an exploration of the earliest fortifications (the legionary fortress, forts, camps, and fortlets) that were built in the area now known as Scotland in the first century. In the first part, it explores the relationship between these sites, and the landscape surrounding them. It looks at the key elements that the Romans considered when choosing where to build their forts, the direction they face, and the relationship with nearby Roman roads and rivers. The second part of the book contains a list of the earliest 120 or so first-century Roman sites, with a summary of the individual landscape setting of each and a brief overview of the evidence used for dating individual sites.

1

Scotland in the First Century

Scotland was invaded by the Romans on at least three occasions. The first was around AD 77–86/90 and is known as the Flavian period. The next took place around AD 139–165, the Antonine period, and led to the construction of the Roman wall running between the firths of Forth and Clyde. The third and final incursion took place between AD 208 and 211 (Severan period). There is some evidence suggesting there may have been additional incursions before and after these main

Kaims Castle Roman fortlet.

periods, but these were not on the same scale as the invasions. In this book, I focus on the 120 or so Roman sites built during the Flavian period, many of which were not subsequently altered or destroyed by later Roman activity, making it easier to examine them in their landscape setting.

We have a good knowledge of the military situation in first-century Scotland thanks to the survival of a book written shortly after the first century. The *Agricola* is a historical account of campaigning in Britain, particularly the north, in the late first century under the Roman governor, who the book is named after. Since its rediscovery in the seventeenth century, the text has influenced our understanding of Roman sites in Scotland, particularly when there has been a lack of datable evidence. In the past there was a tendency to ascribe a first-century origin date to most Roman sites because of the *Agricola,* so it is therefore important to understand the portrayal of northern Britain in it, and how this has influenced Roman Scotland.

Written by his son-in-law, Tacitus, the *Agricola* was probably published around AD 98, shortly after Agricola's death. It's a biased text, written to show off Agricola's military skills, and the book makes grand claims about his achievements while campaigning in Britain. Tacitus claims Agricola was the first to invade Scotland, but there is a growing body of evidence that suggests there were earlier incursions into the north before he arrived in Britain. In another effort to portray his father-in-law as a brilliant military leader, Tacitus claims that all of the fortifications in Scotland were established by Agricola. He also claims that the emperor became jealous and ordered Agricola back to Rome, withdrawing the army from northern Britain. The reality is a little different. Troops were redeployed from elsewhere in Britain to quell uprisings on the Continent, resulting in the soldiers in the north being pulled back south to fill the void.

It isn't until his third and fourth years of campaigning in Britain that Agricola finally secured the lands around the firths of Forth and Clyde, and reached as far north as the Firth of Tay. Tacitus writes that by fortifying the Forth and Clyde, the indigenous tribes were pushed into the northern lands, as if they were different islands. As well as the army, Agricola also had a fleet of ships at his disposal, and while campaigning in the north he tasked the navy with undertaking reconnaissance of local harbours. Tacitus says that once the local population had seen that the Romans were invading from the sea, they turned to armed struggle and attacked Roman sites. Later, he records that Agricola sent the fleet to plunder and attack the local population, before confronting the indigenous tribes at the infamous battle of Mons Graupius, where he battled 30,000 tribesmen and won with minimal losses. In later periods, Roman historians tell us how troublesome for the Empire the indigenous population in northern Britain becomes, often breaching the Antonine and Hadrian's Wall to plunder Imperial territory. Even in the first century, Tacitus, through his description of the battle of Mons Graupius, portrays the tribes as a significant threat, although this is not necessarily seen in the archaeological record.

Tacitus portrays the native tribes as being dangerous and hostile to the invading Romans, which is hardly a surprise given that the military was out to conquer northern Britain for the glory of the senate and people of Rome. But the archaeological evidence is less clear, and there is some indication of coexistence between the Roman army and the indigenous population, although whether or not this was a relationship founded on convenience or hostility is less clear. There are some native sites where archaeologists have argued that the Romans allowed people to continue farming and raising animals because the army needed grain and horses. It was much easier to allow this than for them to import their own grain from far away or install their own farmers, who had no knowledge of the local land or conditions. There are few large indigenous settlements in Scotland at this time, but there are some smaller native forts which are near Roman fortifications, and may have been occupied when the Romans arrived to build their own forts. However, these are quite small and could easily have been taken out by the Roman army if there was a need to. Similarly, a number of indigenous roundhouses have been found but remain unexcavated, immediately next to several Roman forts in Perthshire and Angus, and would not have posed a threat. But while there is some evidence to suggest the Romans tolerated the natives in some parts of the north, elsewhere there does appear to have been an indigenous threat. Indeed, Tacitus tells us about the time that a group of soldiers were attacked by the natives, and there are other Roman writers who tell us about the guerrilla warfare tactics used against the army in Britain. In the second century, when Hadrian's Wall was built across the north of England, the Romans also built a series of fortifications along the northern coast of Cumbria, overlooking the south-west coast of Scotland, where there are a number of indigenous coastal forts. Given that Tacitus tells us that Agricola harassed and raided coastal settlements, it seems likely that there was a continuing threat to the Empire after the first invasion of the north.

2

Fortification Types

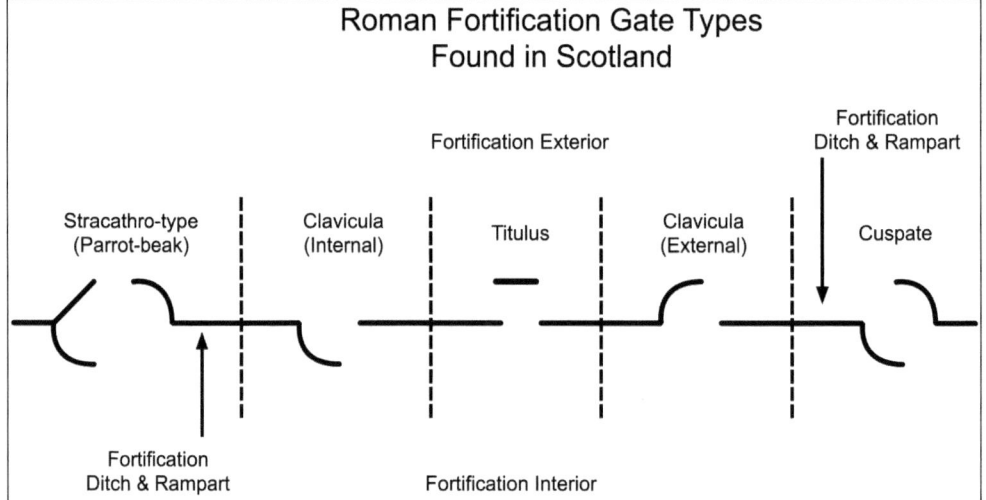

Different types of entrances found on Roman camps in Scotland.

Scotland has an almost unique position in the Roman world as one of the few territories never fully or permanently occupied on a long-term basis in any period. Roman fortifications are found in most geographic areas of the north; from the Solway Firth and the River Tweed in the south, along the fringes of the Highland Faultline, and beyond, to the shores of the Moray Firth. Around 300 confirmed, probable, and possible Roman sites have been identified in Scotland, with a general consensus that most date to one of the three major invasions. However, a substantial number of these sites remain undated. So how do archaeologists date these Roman sites, and what impact does this have on our understanding of them?

Working out the date that Roman sites were founded can be challenging and problematic because of a lack of datable objects recovered from them. Some sites have been dated from surface finds usually recovered during fieldwalking of the fortification. These are finds that have either been brought to the surface, by ploughing or burrowing animals, or lost by a passing Roman 2,000 years ago. While these finds can be dated, and potentially show activity at the site from a specific time period, it really needs excavation to dig below the modern surface to the earlier layers to prove with some certainty that a site was founded in the Roman period.

The *Agricola* has been the default source underpinning the dating of the majority of Roman sites in Scotland before the advent of modern scientific analysis. Most fortifications discovered prior to the twentieth century were usually dated to the first century because Tacitus claimed they were founded by Agricola. Not a particularly helpful approach. Nowadays, archaeologists have much more reliable information about how old artefacts are, backed up by scientific techniques and analysis, enabling them to better date more recently uncovered Roman sites. Camps are particularly challenging to date, partly because so few have been excavated, and when work has been undertaken on these sites, there have been few datable artefacts recovered. Instead, archaeologists tend to date these sites based on one or more of the following methods:

Entrances
Camps have different styles of entrance depending on when they were built, with some distinct designs in use in the first century. Examples of these can be seen in the image above.

Proximity
When a camp is next to another site (usually a fort) known to date to the first century, it is assumed both date to the same period.

Morphology
Where a camp has one or more design features that it shares with another site known to date to the first century, both are assumed to have been built at the same time by the same group of soliders.

Dating
Through finds or scientific methods such as radiocarbon dating.

With hundreds of Roman sites in Scotland, most of which have not been dated using scientific methods, it is not always clear when they were founded or reoccupied; the dating of sites is rarely straightforward. Most of the dating methods outlined above have flaws and can be unreliable, particularly when the evidence for individual fortifications is in conflict, such as a site having two different types of entrance or two conflicting radiocarbon dates.

Legionary Fortress

There is only one legionary fortress established in Scotland in the first century. Located in rural Perthshire, on a plateau overlooking the River Tay, it acted as the regional command headquarters for operations in Scotland; the next nearest fortress was at York, some 250 miles to the south. There is little to be seen at the site today, other than a few ditches and a few stones hidden amongst the undergrowth. Originally, the fortress was built with timber buildings on top of turf foundations, surrounded by a wall of turf, and a ditch. Inchtuthil was similar to other fortresses of the same time, such as Caerleon in Wales and York, and covering an area of 21.5 hectares, 0.5 hectares larger than the latter site. No records or inscriptions from the site survive, and we don't know which legion occupied it, or even the Roman name for the fortress. An integral part of military operations in the north, the fortress would have been the biggest engineering and construction programme ever to have taken place in Scotland at that point. No doubt the indigenous fort at one end of the plateau would have been cleared, along with any rocks and trees, as the engineers laid out the plan of the fortification and began construction. There are also two Roman camps on the peninsula, although these have not been dated but were probably built to house the construction workers. However, before the fortress was completed, Scotland was abandoned by the Romans. Archaeologists know this because during excavation on the fortress site in the twentieth century, they found gaps where there should have been buildings, and the headquarters building (the *principia*) was built from wood and much smaller than the space allocated for it, so it is assumed it would have been rebuilt in stone and much larger had the site not been abandoned.

The remains of the eastern defensive ditch at Inchtuthil legionary fortress.

The site of the camp at Normandykes, now covered by woodland.

Camps

Camps are the most abundant type of Roman fortification found in Scotland, with more than 150 being discovered so far. Sixty-five camps are likely to originate in the first century, although there are many more that are undated and may have been founded in the Flavian period. Traditionally, camps have been interpreted as temporary structures, constructed quickly and occupied briefly, such as overnight or for a few days as the army moved from one place to another. But this is misleading as camps took the best part of a day to construct, and there is increasing evidence from some sites (such as the camp at Kintore in Aberdeenshire) that they were occupied for more than a few nights. Indeed, Tacitus implies camps were occupied through the winter months. Archaeologists have attempted to classify Roman camps into four categories based on their likely purpose. Marching camps are temporary bases of a tented army on campaign or manoeuvres away from their base; most camps fall into this group. Practice camps are small sites that often cluster together (such as at Dalswinton and Lochlands), indicating the exercise grounds and training regimes of the soldiers. Siege camps are enclosures constructed to house troops besieging a nearby indigenous site. The only likely camps of this type can be found at Burnswark in Dumfries and Galloway. Finally, construction camps are temporary, housing soldiers involved in construction of a nearby fortification. Most of those classified as this type have been labelled because of their proximity to the second-century Antonine Wall.

Forts

While camps are portrayed as temporary structures, forts are seen as the opposite: permanent fortifications, usually built from turf with timber super-structures in

The site of Stracathro Roman fort.

first-century Scotland. They also have more extensive rampart and ditch defensive arrangements than camps, although both fortifications share similarities in the internal layout. They were occupied by auxiliary soldiers (as oppose to legionaries), who were effectively paid mercenaries. Thirty-three forts originating in the Flavian period have been identified in Scotland, found across most of the country, with the majority in the Lowlands, and the most northerly site is at Stracathro in Angus – beyond here only camps have been identified. This seems an unusual place to end the chain of permanent fortifications as it leaves open the possibility that those outside the military zone could travel to the east of Stracathro and enter Roman territory without detection. This either indicates an as yet unidentified Roman site near Stonehaven, or that the military strategy was not to control the wider landscape, only the localised area around a fortification.

Fortlets

Fortlets are small fortifications, often unfavourably compared to forts, despite a difference in internal layout, structures, and size. Where we know the internal layout of fortlets in Scotland, they follow the same pattern: an internal space containing buildings (probably barracks), separated by a small road. A rampart and ditch surrounded the internal structures, over which there was a causewayed road. Some fortlets are surrounded by several ditches, and some may have had an annexe (a secure compound) attached to them. While there are examples constructed from stone, those in Flavian Scotland are usually constructed out of turf and timber. Fortlets were generally either positioned between the forts or used to guard areas of strategic importance, such as river crossings or road junctions. Nine Flavian fortlets have been identified in Scotland, with the dating evidence from each site varying in certainty and quality.

Towers

Towers are found on many frontiers across the Empire. In Scotland, they are located around the Gask Ridge in Perthshire, positioned on alternate sides of a road, creating a secure, fortified route with the capacity to signal between the towers and nearby Roman forts. Additional towers are located on various hills in southern Scotland and appear to have formed part of a separate signalling network; the capacity to signal effectively between these sites was limited because of the large distances between them. Datable evidence for all the tower sites is lacking, but the assumption is that most, if not all, belong to the first century, usually because of their closeness and ability to signal to other Flavian sites. The purpose of the chain of fortifications along the Gask Ridge remains unclear. Some archaeologists argue that it is a secure frontier with towers acting as both signal stations and observation posts, while others suggest they provided protection for the supply route to the legionary fortress. A third suggestion is that the system was set up to protect tribes in Fife from attack from those living in the Highlands.

Recreation of a Roman tower at Burgsalach, Germany.

3
Roman Fortress Scotland

Deciding where to place a fortification in the landscape was an important decision for the Romans. The ideal location would have natural terrain that would protect one or more flanks of the fortification. It would be suitably positioned to oversee or control the local population, and it may also protect valuable natural resources. Forts in Scotland are invariably located in fertile parts of the country, and camps are similarly positioned, although the need to establish a temporary encampment while marching through a landscape often led to them being in slightly less ideal locations, or not having natural features to protect the flanks.

Recreation of fort gates at Arbeia fort (South Shields) in north-east England.

The Romans left behind several books or military manuals that state where fortifications should be ideally constructed. One writer, Vegetius, says that soldiers should build a fort in a safe place where there is access to essential resources such as food, water and timber. He goes on to say that if a long-term stay is planned, the site should be salubrious and not be overlooked by high ground or a mountain, as this would give the enemy a tactical advantage. The camp also needs to be the right size for the number of soldiers, not too big or too small, and it should be fortified by hand and nature; in other words, the soldiers should build ramparts and dig ditches or make use of the natural terrain. Another Roman military writer, known as 'Pseudo' Hyginus, compiles a similar list of requirements and says that the encampment should be located on a level or sloping site; failing that, the next best location is on top of a hill. Hyginus notes that the front gate (the *porta praetoria*) should always face the enemy, while the rear entrance (the *porta decumana*) should be placed at the highest point of the site to make the fort look more impressive to anyone viewing it from a distance or on lower slopes. However, it is important to remember that these texts were written after the first century, and therefore should be considered with caution. It is likely that they reflect military practices that were popular at the time of their writing, and perhaps reflect the 'gold standard' in military planning and techniques. Soldiers out in the field would need to be much more adaptable to the local terrain and environment. Fortifications in Scotland tend to reflect this, and are adapted to make best use of the terrain; the camp at Raedykes is the best example of this. Although Roman fortifications in Scotland are not overlooked by mountains, some are built close to hills, upon which are indigenous sites; most of these are undated and may not have been in use at the time of the Flavian incursions. Some 57 per cent of Flavian fortifications are overlooked by hills higher than the one the fortification is on, although relatively few of these are close enough to pose a threat. Therefore, it is unlikely that being overlooked was a significant issue when a site was chosen by the army.

Almost all fortifications make use of the natural landscape for defence, with most built with a river or a steep ravine or valley on one side of the site. In some areas, such as the Scottish Borders, Moray, and parts of Aberdeenshire, where there are fewer rivers and the natural topography lends itself less to defensive features, the fortifications tend to back onto steep hillsides. An example of this can be seen at the camp at Carlops Spittal, where the steep hills on one side of the site provide an additional layer of defence, although the overall location is not ideal as an enemy could fire down on the camp from the hills above. This both demonstrates what aspects of a location were prioritised by the army, but also shows that they were willing to take certain risks. Possibly this was because they did not intend to occupy such sites for a significant length of time, which suggests that this site and others in similar locations were marching camps; those encampments occupied on a temporary basis, perhaps only for a few nights, as the army (and its baggage train) passed through the landscape.

Positioning

By looking at where a Roman fort is placed in the landscape, we can begin to work out its purpose. In early Roman Scotland, 55 per cent of camps, 36 per cent of forts, and 9 per cent of fortlets are located either at the entrance to, or overlooking a valley, or where two or more of these converge. Most of the Flavian fortifications are located next to rivers, with some sites located on the coast at the mouths of rivers, demonstrating a need to control sections of the coast, as well as access to the waterways. This was important if the water network was used for moving troops and supplies to the interior. River confluences, the point where two or more rivers meet, also had strategic importance to the army, with twenty forts, thirty-four camps, and eight Flavian fortlets located near the confluence of at least two rivers. Forts located at the entrance to valleys include Bochastle, Crawford, Dalginross, Easter Happrew, Malling, and Fendoch, although the latter is the only one that can see along the adjacent valley, while the other sites have better views of the immediate surrounding area. The forts at Bertha, Cargill, Dalswinton, Doune Drumquhassle, and Glenlochar are all located overlooking river valleys, and have good views of these. Bertha, Cargill, Glenlochar, and Newstead have poor wider views, with their strength being the visibility of the immediate area, presumably over any river crossings. Loudoun Hill, Milton, and Oakwood have views along the river valleys. Therefore it can be surmised that the forts in Flavian Scotland are located in one of three locations: at the entrance to valleys, where they converge, or overlooking them, poviding visual control over movement through these landscapes.

Some camps have visual control of wider landscapes, while others have oversight of river valleys, and a few are located on, or near to, the coast. Similar to the forts, a large proportion of camps are constructed overlooking valleys, where several converge, or at the entrance to these. The fortlets are located in a range of landscapes, with some, such as Gatehouse of Fleet, Inverquharity, and Kirkland, located at the entrance to valleys, with the former two containing larger rivers. Bankhead and Cargill are located at river confluences, although there are no distinct valleys in these areas. Cargill and Gatehouse have limited views of the wider area, which suggests they may have been guarding river crossings. Castle Greg, Glenbank, and Kaims Castle are the three fortlets that are located on roads. Notably, these sites have the best views, and this may be because their role was to protect the road rather than to control the wider landscape. There have been few attempts to identify river crossings, or even the termini of roads on river banks. The limited evidence suggests that fortifications were not generally orientated towards river crossings, even when they are located in close proximity to these, and this may indicate that the fortification was constructed before the road, or a formalised crossing point, such as a bridge, was in place.

Orientation

Determining the orientation of a fortification is dependent on identifying key features of the site, such as the *principia*, the central headquarters building in a fort or fortress, and the first structure soldiers and visitors would see on entering a fortification through the main gate of the site. If the layout outline of the *principia* can be established, then so can the orientation of the overall fort. While occasionally the shape of fortifications varies, often this is because, like camps, the design of the site, in particular the defences, makes use of the surrounding terrain. Forts in Scotland are overwhelmingly similar in shape and layout, making the orientation easier to determine if additional features can be identified. These include the long/short axis, internal roads, and/or the gates as seen in the image below. Identifying camp orientation has a different set of challenges because of their relatively temporary nature. Often they don't survive as well as forts because of the construction methods and materials used. When only partial defences of a camp are known, it can make identifying the orientation more difficult. Fortlets do not have an orientation in the same way as camps and forts because they lack the same internal layout and structures that help to determine the direction the site faces. Instead, it is the positioning of the single entranceway and what it faces that determine the direction of a fortlet.

The Roman military writers tell us that fortifications should face a certain direction for both practical and symbolic reasons. They say that a site should either face east, towards the enemy, or in the direction of advance. It is Vegetius, writing in a period where Christian worship was increasingly common, who states that the site should face east, but as the fortifications in Scotland were built before the widespread adoption of Christianity, it is unlikely that this advice was practised in northern Britain at this time. The reasoning behind orientating fortifications in the direction of advancement is less clear. Perhaps it was a practical consideration, making it easier for soldiers to leave in the direction they would move in, but this seems redundant given the baggage train for the army could be up to 10 kilometres long. The final direction that the Roman writers says the fort should be facing is towards the enemy. There might be a symbolic purpose behind this. Indigenous people seeing a Roman fort for the first time would be amazed and astounded, having never seen anything like this before. Perhaps building the fort to face the enemy was a deliberate, psychological attempt to intimidate anyone who might challenge the Imperial war machine. However, not many of the early Roman sites are following the instructions set out by the Roman writers; few fortifications face east, and even expanding this definition to include those facing north-east or south-east, the numbers remain statistically low. The number of fortifications (excluding fortlets) facing either east, north-east, or south-east is twenty out of

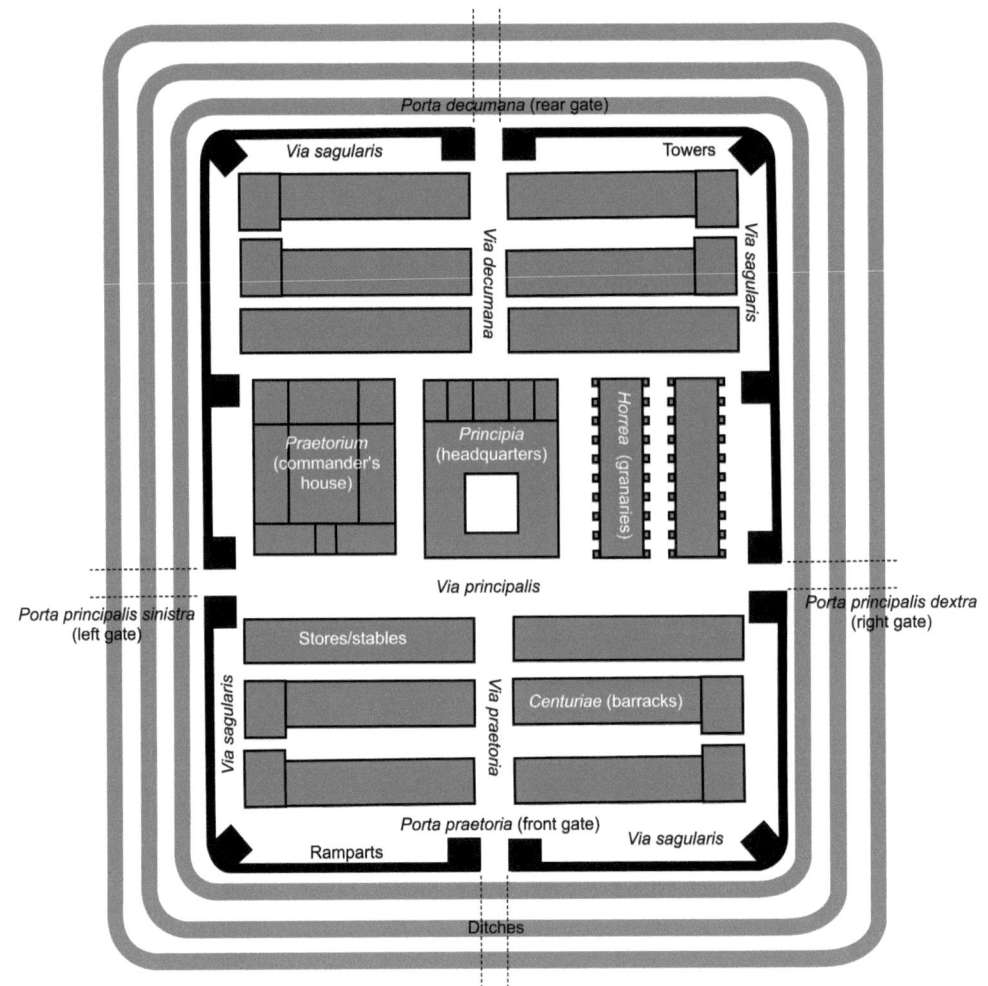

Plan of a typical Roman fort.

ninety-eight sites; only seven of these face due east. Out of all of the Flavian sites, only the forts at Bertha and Ardoch are facing the direction of advancement.

So are early Roman sites in Scotland built facing the enemy? The relationship between the Romans and the indigenous population remains unclear. Were the native occupants of hill forts and promontory forts seen as the 'enemy' or not? Only 1 per cent of the early Roman forts and camps are facing indigenous hill forts, although a further 17 per cent could be facing these (the orientation of the Roman sites are undetermined). Meanwhile, 78 per cent of the first-century Roman fortifications are not facing indigenous sites. Curiously, most of the indigenous forts next to the Roman sites are very small, mainly oval, and all less than 0.4 hectares in size. It remains possible that some of them were occupied and were perceived to pose a threat to the Roman military.

4

Roman Control of Scottish Landscapes

The soldiers had good views of the wider landscape from some Roman sites, but more often than not these could be limited by the surrounding terrain. This implies that the army was less concerned about seeing longer distances. Their priority was being able to see the immediate area around a site. Locating a fortification in such a prominent position in the landscape would have a major psychological impact on the indigenous population who would have to pass by the site. This image, and the power it represents, would essentially become a form of defence for the site.

As previously noted, fortifications are located in, or overlooking, valleys, which indicates that they were placed there to control the immediate landscape. Visibility from these sites can be poor and not overly extensive, but would nonetheless have given the Roman army significant advantages in surveying and controlling strategic points in the landscape. This suggests these fortifications have a role in managing movement through these key areas, rather than purely existing to prevent a hostile force attacking Roman territory. The army did not have the capacity to secure every valley in Scotland, and instead opted to place fortifications in key strategic locations where the natives needed to pass by when moving from one place to another. This can be seen with the sites along the edge of the Highlands (which Abernethy called the glen-blocking forts). These were not necessarily intended to act as launchpads for further invasion of the Highlands, nor were they intended to block all movement into Imperial territory, as they (like many fortification sites) could easily be circumvented with alternative routes through the landscape taken, such as crossing over hills or using old trackways. But inevitably, if another path was taken, and which followed a river valley, a Roman fortification would be encountered at some point and there would be little opportunity to escape military scrutiny. Essentially, the primary role of forts is not to control the entirety of the wider landscape; this is a by-product of their presence in a location. Their key role is to restrict and manage movement through certain areas and by making the population pass by fortifications, giving the army an opportunity to collect taxes, goods or whatever else took their fancy.

Encouraging traffic to move through the landscape using preferred routes is demonstrated at a number of other Flavian fortifications, with the clearest example from the fort at Crawford, which is facing south-east down the Clyde valley with views of the approaching Roman road from Carlisle. However, it is also positioned at the entrance of another valley, to the east, beyond which is an indigenous Iron Age fort. Even when fortifications face specific features, particularly river crossings or the road network, it is all about control and funnelling traffic past the Roman sites. Ardoch is one of the very few forts not to be located in or near a valley, but is at the southern extremity of the road running over the Gask Ridge. One reason for the construction of the fort in this location may be to control access to a pre-existing route, later adopted by the Romans. The importance of this route is reflected in the positioning of the fortlets of Kaims Castle and Glenbank, both of which have their entrances

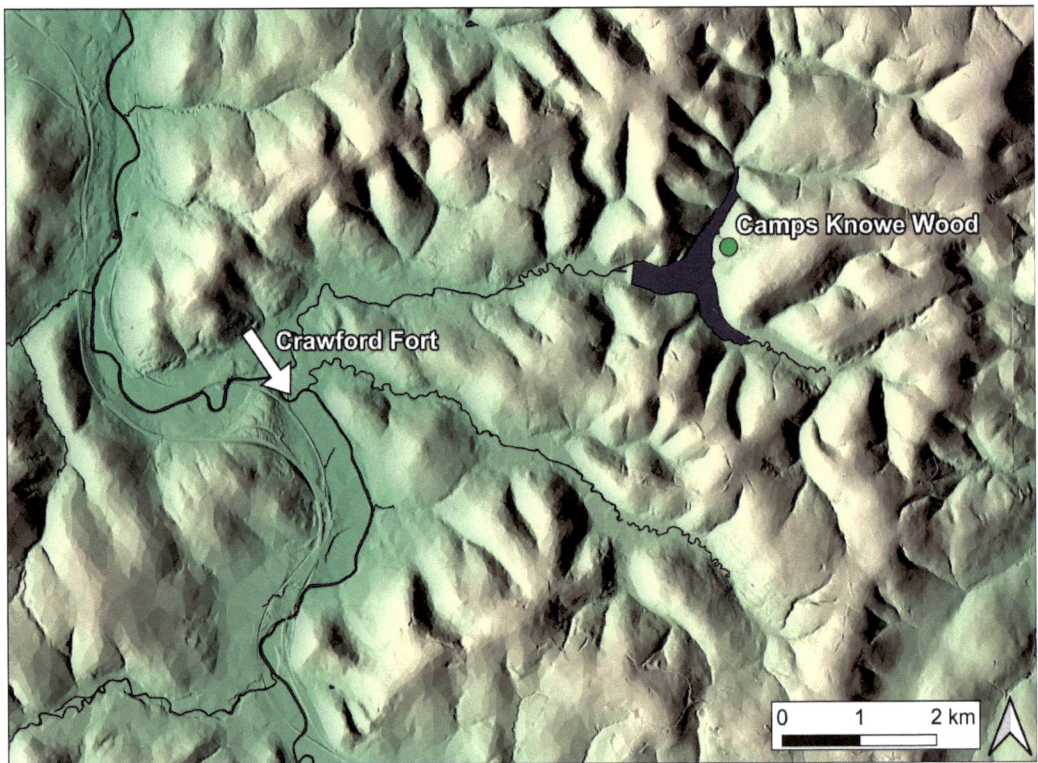

The fort at Crawford overlooking the valley to the south and blocking access to the valley leading to Camps Knowe Wood in the east.

facing directly onto the road, which suggests a role in managing this ancient route and the traffic using it.

The Roman military strategy appears to have comprised a mixture of campaigning, evidenced through the establishment of marching camps, attempts to secure the region through the construction of permanent fortifications, and the placing of these in strategic locations. They use some camps to fulfil the function of forts in controlling movement routes, both inland and on the coast, may reflect the need to quickly establish fortifications in certain locations, but the brief nature of the occupation of north Britain meant that most of these were never replaced with permanent forts. The military strategy was therefore not to stop all movement through the landscape, as implied by the notion of 'glen-blocking' forts. Such a strategy would have been impossible to maintain in a region with so many circumventable valleys, hills, and mountains and it would have been impossible to police them all, and unnecessary. Instead, the aim of the army was to control the movement of the indigenous population through the landscape, achieved by constructing Roman fortifications either in, or at the entrance to, these movement routes. By doing this, they would exert both visual control and authority over the indigenous population, and negate the need to control the entirety of the Scottish landscape.

5
The Early Fortifications

This section of the book covers all the confirmed and likely first-century Flavian fortification sites in Scotland. Each entry details the type of fortification, the orientation by degree and cardinal direction (where known), along with the National Grid Reference. This is followed by a summary of the topographical setting and positioning of the fortifications, a description of the orientation, and a summary of the dating evidence for each site.

Aberdeenshire

Burnfield
Camp | Orientation: Unknown | NJ 540 476

Burnfield is constructed on a hillside, making use of a steeper hill to the south-east to protect that flank of the camp, while also making use of the valley of the River

Deveron to the north-west. Views from the camp are limited, mainly restricted to the north side of the river valley. The site is particularly close to the camps at Muiryfold (4.59 Roman miles) and Auchinhove (5.97 Roman miles), both in Moray. With only the north-east and south-west sides of this fort identified, it is not possible to speculate which direction the camp faced, although it could be towards a river crossing on the north-eastern side of the site. Burnfield was discovered from the air by Ralston in 1982 and excavated by him with St Joseph. Although no datable evidence for this site has been uncovered, it is speculated to be Flavian due to its location and its comparable size with the camps at Auchinhove and Ythan Wells.

Glenmailen (Ythan Wells)
Camp I | Orientation: Unknown | NJ 655 381
Camp II | Orientation: 99° (North) | NJ 6603 3847

The partially overlapping camps at Ythan Wells are located above the River Ythan, constructed on a steep hillside and overlooked by hills to the north-east and south-west. Both camps make use of a small river valley (the Dry Burn), which runs to the west and north, with camp II facing the River Ythan. The waterways appear

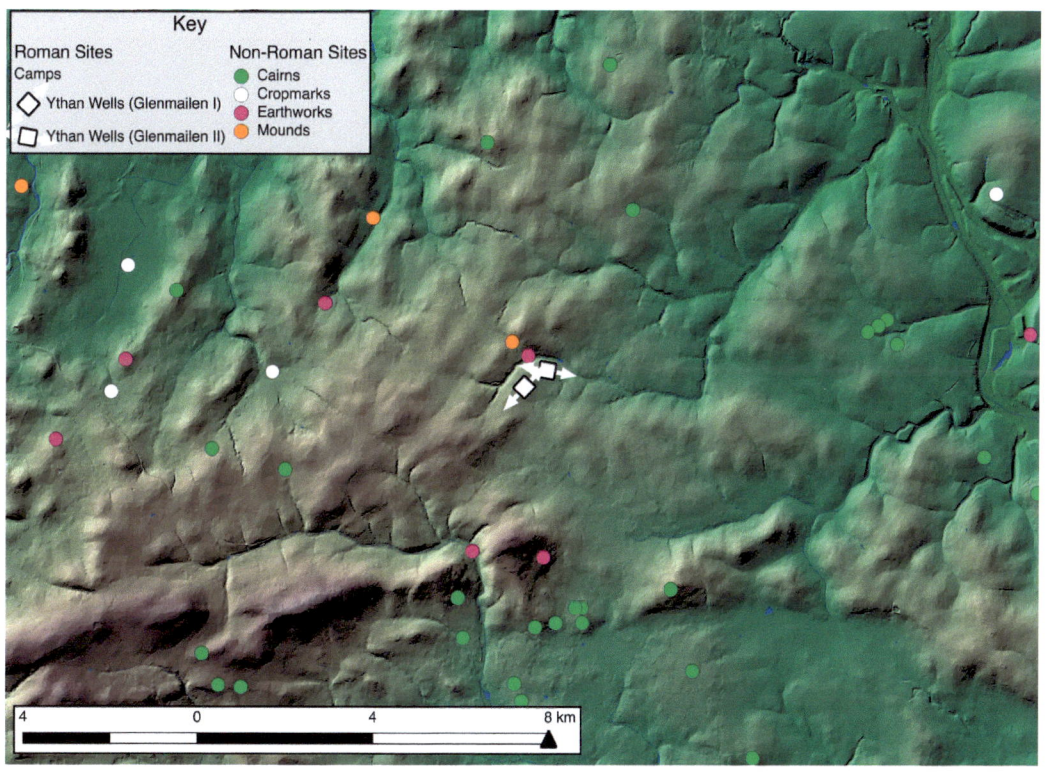

Archaeological features around Glenmailen (Ythan Wells) camps.

to have been altered through agricultural works, and may follow slightly different courses than in the first century. Camp I is almost trapezoidal, but possibly faces north-east or south-west and possibly towards the Ythan. Excavation has shown that camp I is built on top of camp II, indicating that it came later. There is an absence of more precise dating for the site, but as both camps seem to form part of a chain of early fortifications running in a line through north-east Scotland, they are assumed to date to the first century. The dating is strengthened as camp II has Stracathro-style gates, which are seen on other first-century sites.

Kintore
Camp | Orientation: Unknown | NJ 78739 16232

Kintore camp is constructed on a gentle rise, now mainly covered with modern housing and industrial works. To the east of the camp is the River Don, while several minor rivers flow nearby, although the modern Ordnance Survey map indicates their courses have been altered. The site would have been overlooked to the south-east, and there would have been limited views to the north and south. There is little natural topography in the area, other than the Don, to aid defence of the camp. The camp is mainly playing card shaped, although the southern end

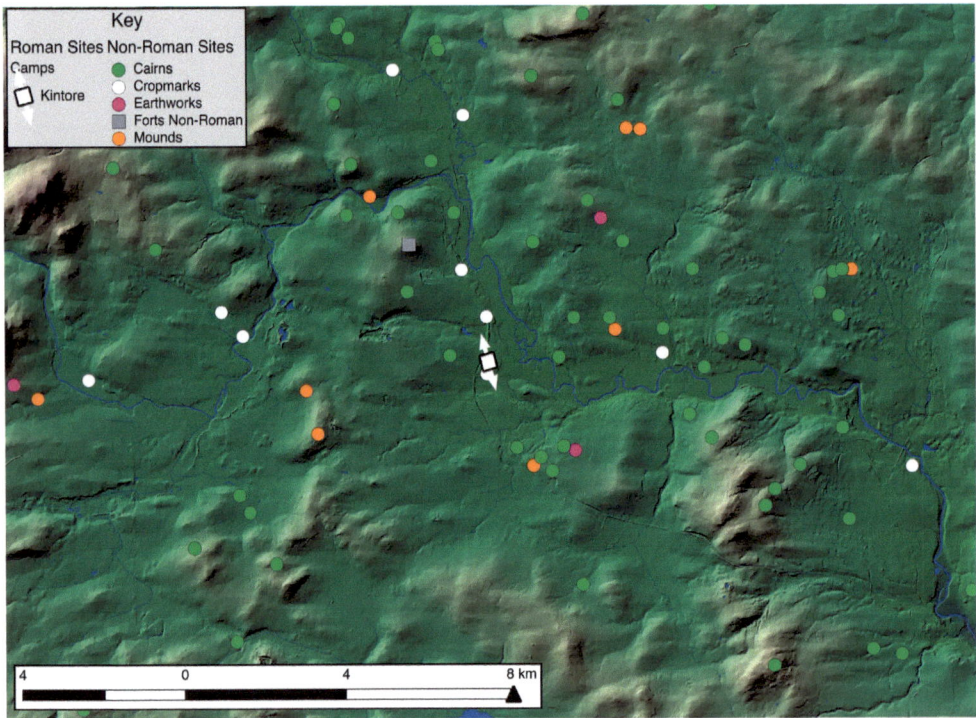

Archaeological features arround Kintore camp.

is slightly wider than the northern half, and it faced north-west or south-east. In the latter direction are a series of twenty-seven cairns, while to the north-east lies Fullerton, a promontory fort (NJ 7810 1840). Identified from cropmarks, the indigenous fort has partially been destroyed by the construction of the railway and modern works, but there appears to be traces of two ditches, and it covers an area of 0.32 hectares, with a roundhouse and possibly a souterrain within the interior, but no datable artefacts have been recorded. There is further evidence of the importance of the location of Kintore from discoveries of Iron Age pottery at the site and a possible prehistoric timber circle beneath the Roman camp. Kintore camp was first recorded at the end of the eighteenth century, but extensive, modern excavation of the site did not take place until the latter part of the twentieth century, when the camp was threatened by development. The excavations have yielded radiocarbon dates, which indicate a late first-century occupation of the site.

Logie Durno

Camp | Orientation: 342° (North) | NJ 6985 2718

The area around Logie Durno lacks a suitably large, level space on which to build a camp, and so the fortification was constructed over a steep hill. The River Urie flows to the south-west of the site, and the camp defences make use of this natural topography. Although the camp had good views to the south-west, these were limited in a northerly direction. Although not strictly playing card shaped, the northern defences of the camp turn around 20 degrees to the north on the long axis to take advantage of the topography. From the position of the gates, it indicates that the site was facing north. To the south-east was a burial cairn, now destroyed. Excavation has failed to indicate an origin date for the camp, and despite the size of the site suggesting that it could belong to the large expeditionary force that invaded Scotland in the third century, the general consensus is that it belongs to the chain of fortifications established in the north-east under Agricola. There has been some speculation that the site was particularly large (57 hectares) as it was used as a base for the battle of Mons Graupius.

Milltimber

Camp | Orientation: Unknown | NJ 860 006

A relatively new discovery, the camp at Milltimber was discovered during construction of the Aberdeen bypass. Located on the River Dee, a little way upriver of the camp at Normandykes, it made use of the waterway to protect its southern flank. The site would have been overlooked by higher ground on the north and south sides, across the Dee. The site may have been chosen because of its proximity to the river, which would have enabled quick access for shipping sailing in from the North Sea, as well as to Normandykes camp further upriver. Radiocarbon dating during excavations gave an occupation date of the first century.

Normandykes
Camp | Orientation: 80° (East) | NO 82970 99380

Normandykes makes use of the natural landscape, being visibly located on the summit of a hill. Facing either east or west, it makes full use of the surrounding defensive topography, particularly the valley of the River Dee to the south. Several streams originate on the hill, so a fresh water supply would have been available, while the 1860 map of Normandykes highlights a Roman well to the immediate east of the camp. By the 1900s, the well was noted on the map as being Norman's Well, which could be a corruption of the word Roman. To the north of the site is the Temple Burn. Normandykes is playing card shaped, with the highest gate being on the west, indicating that the camp faces east. While the site may have been constructed at a crossing point over the Dee, it is also close to the newly discovered camp at Milltimber. Excavated several times in the twentieth century, no datable artefacts were found during these works. The site is presumed to be Flavian because of its location as part of the north-eastern chain of fortifications.

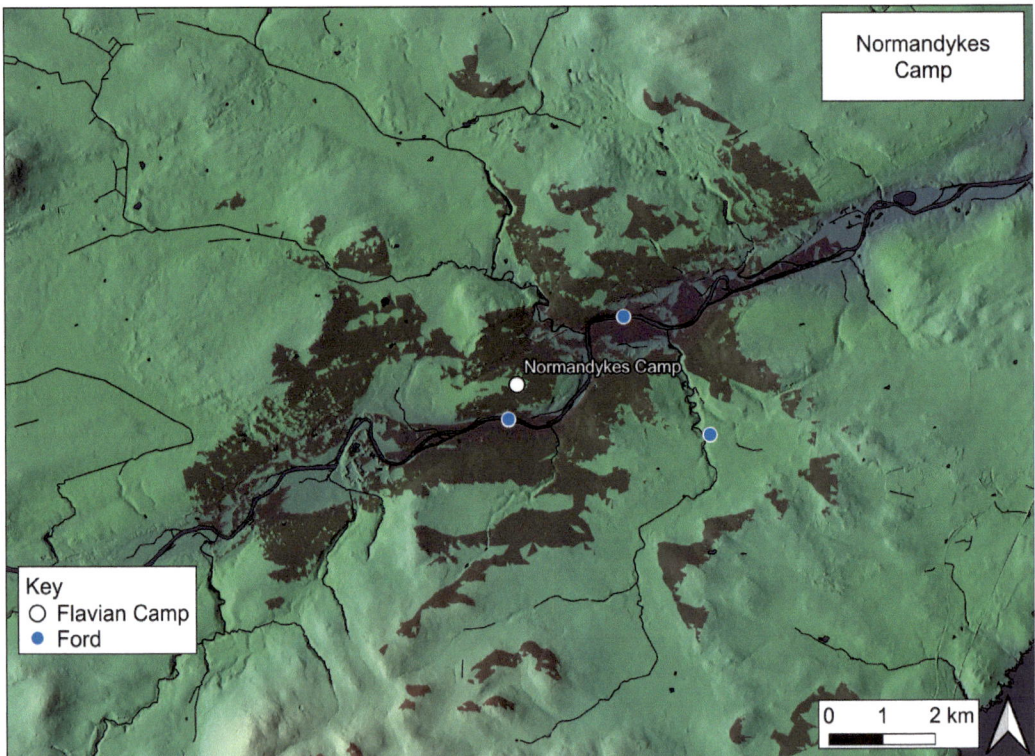

Visible area (dark shading) from Normandykes camp.

Raedykes

Camp | Orientation: Unknown | NO 841 902

The layout of the defences at Raedykes is unusual and makes use of the natural topography of Gallows Hill, itself within the perimeter of the camp defences. As such, the camp has a non-traditional shape, making it difficult to draw any conclusions about how defensive the site was, or what threats it faced. The Cowie Water runs to the south, with a number of burns in the vicinity of Raedykes. In places, the defensive ditches have been cut through rock, something seen at the indigenous site Quinloch Muir by Drumquhassle fort. While the site does have some good views, the surrounding landscape is particularly hilly, restricting visibility of approaching people. Given the unusual shape of the camp, the internal layout is unclear, and it is not possible to work out the orientation of the site. Although this camp has *tituli* at the entrances on the eastern side, there has been some debate regarding dating, not helped by a lack of datable evidence. The general consensus is that it is first century, forming part of the north-east chain of sites, but there has been speculation that it may have been founded in the second or third centuries.

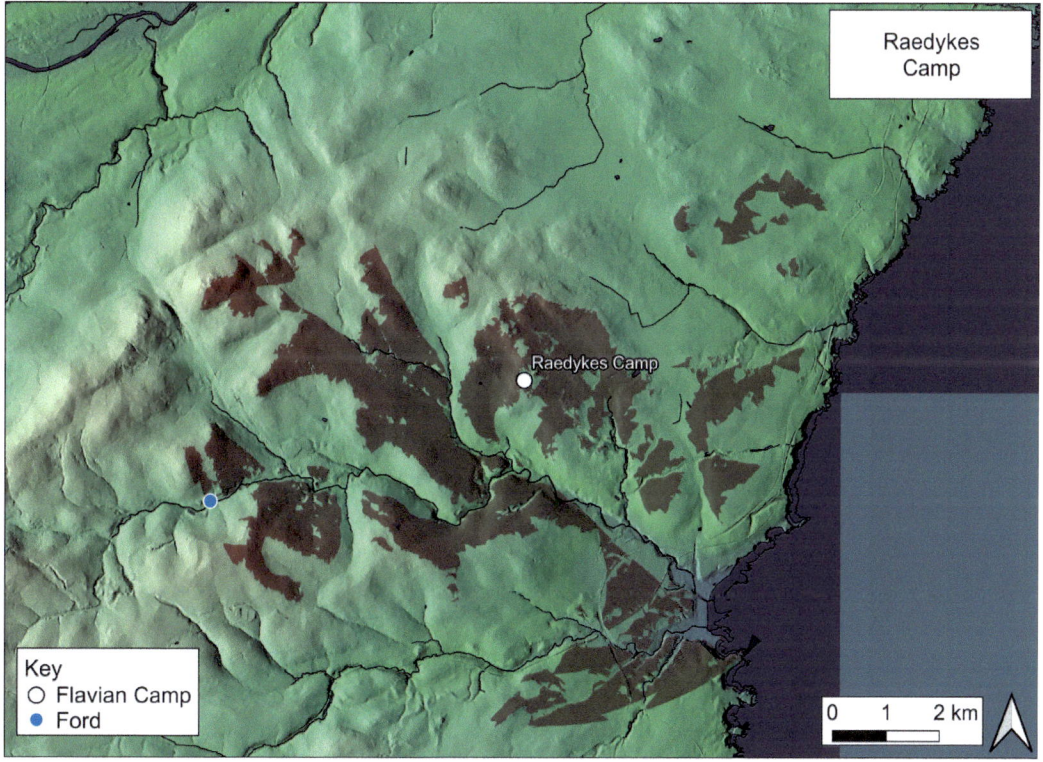

Visible area (dark shading) from Raedykes camp.

Angus

Cardean
Fort | Orientation: 303° (North-west) | NO 28900 46000

Located on a rise between the Dean Water and the River Isla, close to the confluence of these two waterways, the fort defensively uses the river valley of the former. On the north side, LiDAR (aerial laser scanning) analysis suggests that the Isla may have originally run closer to the fort, although both rivers have subsequently moved course and eroded the surrounding terrain. The site commands excellent views of the surrounding area, particularly to the north-east where aerial photography has indicated several rectilinear and curvilinear features, and a souterrain to the north-east. Survey work at the fort has indicated that the site is orientated north-west, facing the Isla, and potentially a crossing point, although no stretches of road or Roman sites have been identified on the opposite bank. Instead, the road has been recorded heading north-west, away from the fort. Any evidence for a crossing may have been obliterated by the route of a nineteenth-century railway line and bridge that is by the north end of the fort. The site was initially dated to the first century when Flavian pottery was recovered during excavations in the 1960s.

Site of Cardean fort.

Site of Dun camp.

Dun
Camp | Orientation: Unknown | NO 6890 5959

Located on the northern shores of Montrose Bay, Dun camp is located on low-lying ground, with a ridge of hills surrounding the site to the north. The bay provides an additional layer of defence for the site, although it is only 10 metres above sea level so may have flooded at certain times of the year. Dun commands excellent views over Montrose Bay to the south. With only the northern gate identified, and the southern defences unidentified, it is not possible to calculate the orientation, although the highest gate is on the north side, suggesting that the camp may have faced south. The camp has *tituli* on the south-east side, a feature common in first-century camps. Pottery discovered during excavations has indicated activity between AD 70 and 90.

Inverquharity
Fortlet | Orientation: 22° (North) | NO 40510 58144
Camp | Orientation: 204° (South-west) | NO 40660 58000

Both sites are located on a hill overlooking the Prosen Water to the north, while the Quharity Burn runs to the south. The camp is located near the confluence of the Prosen Water with the River South Esk, and overlooks the meeting of the waters. There is evidence of erosion on the northern side, although it is unknown when this happened. The best views for both sites are to the north, towards to the river. The fortlet does not appear to be orientated towards a specific site, but the camp is facing what is speculated to be three souterrains. The camp is presumed to be Flavian based on its parrot-beak entrances. No datable evidence for the fortlet has been uncovered, but it is assumed to be of Flavian date due to the similarities and proximity to other sites of this period in the wider area.

Stracathro

Fort | Orientation: Unknown | NO 61700 65750
Camp | Orientation: Unknown | NO 61370 65610

The fort and camp at Stracathro are located on flat ground, although the former appears to be on a headland, with the Cruick Water to the south, the West Water on the north, and the confluence of these with the River North Esk to the east. Both sites make use of this natural topography for defence in what would otherwise be a wide, flat and unprotected landscape. Both sites command extensive 180° views to the north, with the fort orientated towards the confluence (assuming this is the direction it faces). There is a tradition of the confluence being the location of the King's Ford river crossing, although there is no evidence on the ground to indicate if this ever existed. To the south-east of the fort there is Brawl's Well, a natural spring that formed a healing well.

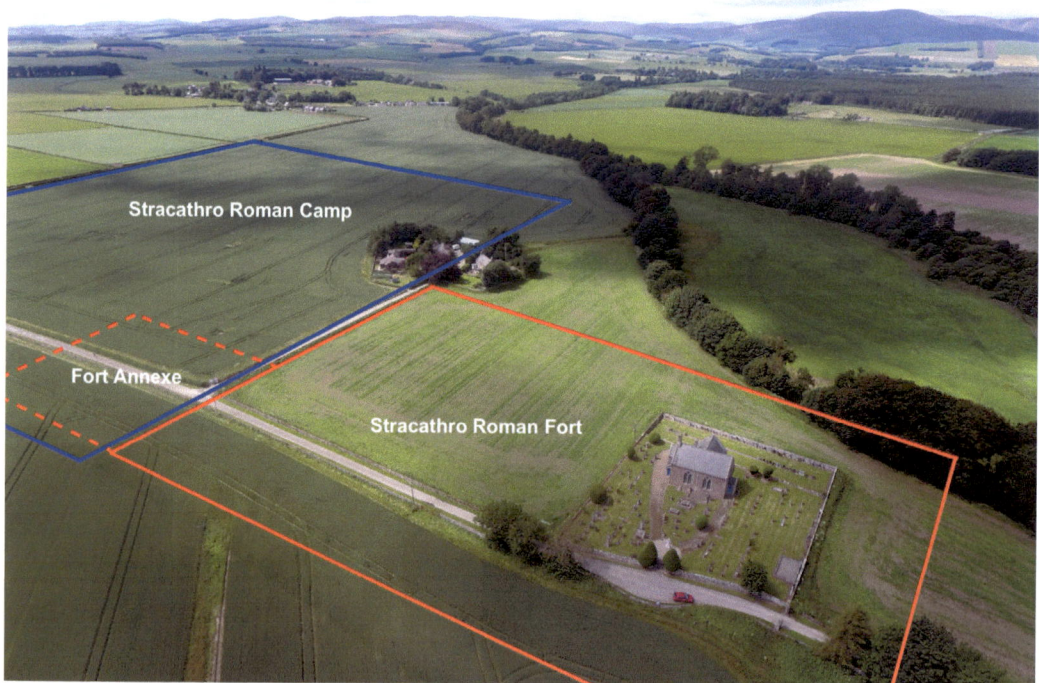

While the origins of it are unknown, it may have supplied the fort, but as it is lower than the fort plateau, water would have had to be conveyed uphill. It is unclear which direction the fort faces, but excavation in the twentieth century indicates it is either south-west or north-east. Geophysical survey in 2012 showed some of the interior of the site, suggesting the fort faced north-east, although only excavation can confirm this. Not enough of the camp defences survive to postulate the orientation of this site, but anecdotally, it appears to face south-west, although this is away from the strategically important river confluence and potential crossing point. Excavations have yielded pottery and coinage, giving a late first-century date for the fort, supported by the geophysical surveys that indicated the fort had parrot-beak entrances (otherwise known as Stracathro-type). The camp is assumed to also date to this period due to its proximity to the fort.

Ayrshire

Ayr
Camp | Orientation: Unknown | NS 348 213

Recently discovered during construction works on a new school, the camp at Ayr is unusual because it does not appear to have any defensive ramparts and ditches. Instead, it was identified through radiocarbon dating of ovens, which dated usage of these to the Flavian period. Like many such sites, the camp was constructed on the banks of the River Ayr, making use of the waterway for natural protection on the southern side.

Girvan Mains
Camp: East | Orientation: Unknown | NX 19000 99106
Camp: West | Orientation: Unknown | NX 1870 9900

Located on relatively flat ground, though overlooked by hillier ground to the south-east, both sites take advantage of the natural defences of the Girvan Water, which flows into the Irish Sea nearby. The next nearest Flavian fortification is some 40 miles away (Glenluce or Loudoun Hill), which either implies further lost sites or that this was used as a stop-off point for coastal traffic, though no harbour has been found. Antiquarian accounts imply that there may have been Roman sites further along the coast at Largs and Ardrossan, although these remain unconfirmed. While the long/short axis have been identified in the east camp, the position of the gates has not been recorded, indicating that the camp faced east or west. The northern defences have not been identified on the west camp, so it is not possible to discern the direction it is facing. Given that both camps had good visibility over the Irish Sea, it is quite possible that they were facing in this direction. Although the east camp, which was discovered from the air in the 1970s, is assumed to be Flavian, there is no datable evidence to support this assertion. The west camp, which intersects the east site, was excavated shortly after discovery and a fragment of first-century glass was found at the bottom of the defensive ditch.

Loudoun Hill

Fort | Orientation: South-east or North-east | NS 6059 3712

The fort is a lone site in the middle of Ayrshire, and has been assumed to be 'guarding' the Roman road on an east–west route, although most of this route has not been traced on the ground. The fort was located on a level platform overlooking an east–west valley and in the shadow of Loudoun Hill, which itself is the site of an undated hill fort on it. Sadly, the fort site was destroyed by quarrying in the mid-twentieth century, but was subjected to a brief series of excavations as the quarry encroached upon the fortification. It only took seventeen years from the

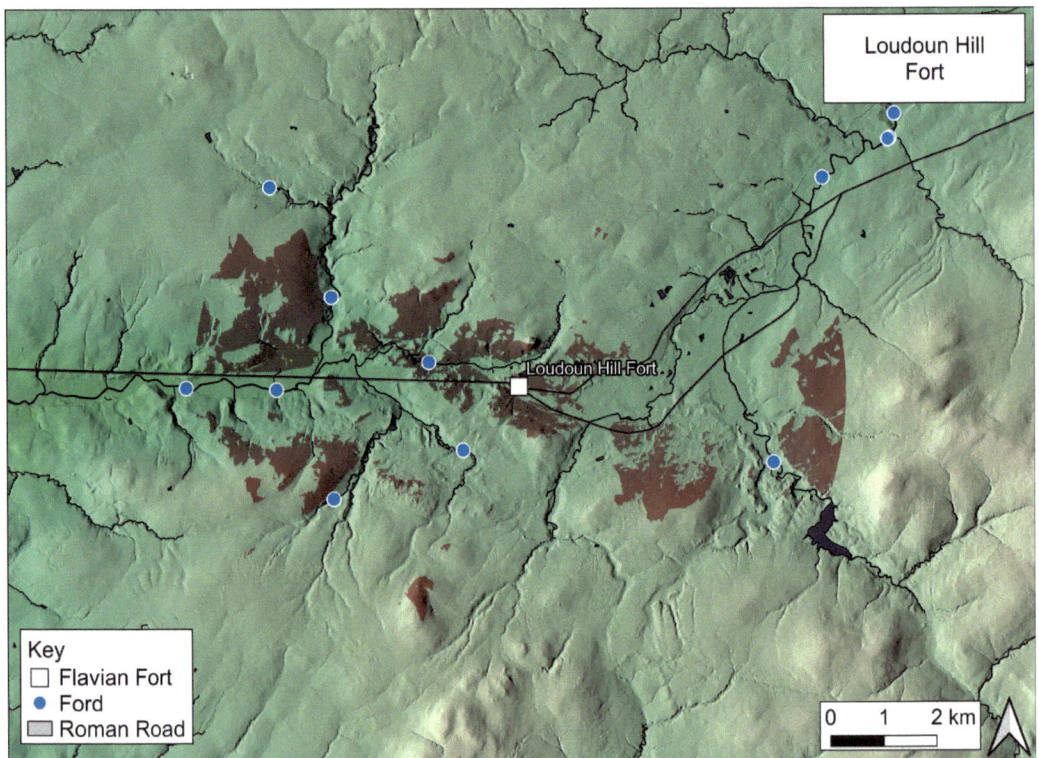

Visible area (dark shading) from Loudoun Hill fort.

site being discovered to it being destroyed by 1955. The excavator, J. K. St Joseph, left few records of the excavations, and the published accounts are lacking in detail, leaving many questions about the site unanswered. The size and shape of the site is peculiar, although it is not possible to say if the design was influenced by the natural topography of the area. St Joseph drew plans of the site during different periods of occupation, although during the Flavian activity at the site, the plan appears to show a half-size fort, something that is occasionally seen at fortifications on the Continent. There is the possibility that St Joseph included buildings from different periods in his haste to record the site, or the plans may show a fort reduced in size. The layout of the fort is fairly unique in Scotland, and the positioning of the internal structures suggests the fort could face south-east or north-east. With the destruction of the fort and its immediate surroundings, questions about the orientation, layout and phasing of the site remain unanswered, and so Loudoun Hill should not be held up as a good example of a Flavian fortification.

The fort was recorded as early as the eighteenth century, although it then disappears from history until its rediscovery by St Joseph, who came across it when tracing the Roman road in the area. This was followed up by Glasgow Archaeological Society, who undertook small excavations on site, but by 1942 the site was being encroached upon by gravel quarrying, which led to the rescue excavations. During this work, St Joseph uncovered evidence for four periods of Flavian occupation and one short-lived phase of Antonine activity, after which the site was deliberately demolished. Dating for the latter period came from pottery, indicating that the lower levels were pre-Antonine and probably Flavian; there were several similarities in features found from the first period of activity to other early sites, such as Birrens.

Dumfries and Galloway

Beattock (Bankend and Barnhill)
Camp (Bankend) | Orientation: Unknown | NT 08488 02049
Fortlet (Possible) (Barnhill) | Orientation: Unknown | NT 08512 02851

Located in the bottom of a wide river valley, the camp and possible first-century fortlet (which lies within the north-west corner of the camp) are located close to the sites at Milton, which are also believed to be Flavian in date. The A74(M), a main arterial route from England to central Scotland, runs through the Clyde Valley, and it is likely that this has been an important arterial route for centuries. Views up the valley to the north are good, but are blocked to the south by a slight rise. With only two sides of the camp known, it is not possible to identify the direction that it was facing, although there has been some suggestion that it faced the point where the Roman road from Carlisle crossed the Evan Water. However, the road has been traced here, and the camp is unlikely to be facing a crossing unless the line of the road or river was different when the camp was constructed, but this seems unlikely. During excavation of the fortlet, a single entrance was uncovered on the eastern side, which indicates that the fortlet faced the road and river. There is some debate on whether or not the Roman road was built under the direction of Agricola, or one of his predecessors. The camp has parrot-beak entrances, which suggests it belongs to the Flavian period. Excavation at the site indicated the fortlet was beneath part of the camp defences, suggesting that it is earlier, dating to some point in the first century.

Birrens
Fort | Orientation: 167° (South) | NY 21900 75180
Camp (Possible) | Orientation: 255° (West) | NY 22462 75028

Birrens is the site of the first large-scale excavation of a Roman fort in Scotland in 1896. The sites are overlooked by hills to the north, next to small river valleys. The fort, and the possible camp, are located at crossing points over the Mein Water, although this assumption is based on the projected route of the road, rather than the confirmed course. The fort site is particularly complex, with remains dating to the Antonine, Hadrianic, and Flavian periods. Beneath this are the remains of a first-century enclosure, sometimes interpreted as an early Flavian fort, which is at a different angle to the later fortifications, facing around 150° or south-east, away

Birrens Roman fort.

from the nearby river. The nineteenth-century excavations uncovered the *principia*, indicating that the fort faced south. The main road into Scotland probably runs to the west of the sites and may date to the early Flavian period, meaning that the camp or enclosure under the fort would also be next to the road. The camp would appear to be facing towards the road, which is around 230 metres away. Most of the defences of the camp have been identified, along with a possible gap indicating a gate on the southern side. With the highest gate on the short axis on the eastern side, it is probable that the camp faced west. The fort was first recorded in 1726, and was excavated at the end of the nineteenth century, along with several times throughout the twentieth century. Datable artefacts from the site were not recovered until the 1930s, and reaffirmed in the 1960s. The camp, which is to the east of the fort, is assumed to be Flavian because of its proximity to the fort, and as it has a *tituli*-style gate associated with early sites.

Broomholm
Fort | Orientation: Unknown | NY 3786 8145

Identified from aerial photographs, the fort is located on the slope of a hill overlooking the Tarras Water and associated river valley, a little north-east of its confluence with the River Esk. A drawing of the site was plotted in the 1950s, based on excavations, although analysis of the original aerial photographs suggests that only the corner of the fort is visible. Further analysis through geophysical survey or LiDAR may confirm if there are additional features on the ground, and if they are connected to the fortification. The lack of identifiable defences means it is not possible to calculate the orientation, although the site is next to the River Esk and a possible circular indigenous fort, Broomholm Knowe (NY 3778 8124), to the south-west of the Roman fortification. Coins found around 1782 indicated first-century activity in the area, a date supported by pottery uncovered during limited excavations in the 1950s. The excavators concluded that there were three periods of occupation, including two from the Flavian period, and one Hadrianic.

Dalswinton
Fort (Bankfoot) | Orientation: Unknown | NX 93301 84101
Fort (Bankhead I) | Orientation: 126° (South-east) | NX 93310 84850
Forts (Bankhead II) | Orientation: 212° (South-west) | NX 93310 84850
Camp (Bankfoot I) | Orientation: Unknown | NX 93440 84081
Camp (Bankfoot II) | Orientation: Unknown | NX 93678 83837

Dalswinton is complex, with multiple fortifications, most of which are likely to date to the Flavian period, indicating it had importance in the first century, such as protecting a strategic crossing over the River Nith. The forts are constructed on a ridge overlooking the river, while the camps are located on the floor of the river valley. The sites are all overlooked to the north-east. The Bankhead forts were initially identified from the air by St Joseph and excavated by Richmond and St Joseph. Using a combination of aerial photographs and excavation, they produced a plan of the forts, noting that there were two Flavian forts on the site. The excavation had a limited scope, and the excavators relied heavily on aerial photographs to interpret the layout and features of the sites. Geophysical work in the early twenty-first century indicated the layout reflected the aerial photographs. It seems probable that Bankhead I fort faces south-east, while Bankhead II faces south-west; this is assuming that both sites follow the more common layout of the *principia* facing the *porta praetoria* on a long axis site, rather than the short axis (as happens at the forts at Crawford and Loudoun Hill). Bankhead II, which is orientated towards a bend in the Nith, is facing the undated Roman camps at Ellisland (NX 9287 8421). It is not possible to identify the orientation of the Bankfoot fort because of the lack of internal structures, while the incomplete defences make it difficult to identify the orientation of the camps.

There has been a lack of firm, datable evidence from any of these sites. Little is known about the fort at Bankfoot, although some suggest that it had two phases of occupation, both being Flavian. As the camps are on the flood plain, then they were likely to be earlier than the Bankhead forts, but still from the Flavian period, although there is the caveat that having four sites from the same period in close proximity is rare. Camp I, the largest, is assumed to be Flavian because of the Stracathro-style gate in the south side and because of the proximity to the forts from that period. The same reasoning is used for the dating of camp II, which is smaller and has a similar gate on the north-east side.

Denholm (Eastcote)
Camp | Orientation: Unknown | NT 5432 1781

Located at a bend in the River Teviot, the camp was built on the flood plain, although the site has been eroded by the waterway in the past. Only part of the defences are known, so it is not possible to say which way the site faced, but it may have been towards an unlocated crossing point over the Teviot. Due to similarities in size with other camps, and its squarish dimensions, it is assumed to be Flavian.

Drumlanrig (including Islafoot)
Fort | Orientation: 332° (North-west) | NX 85426 98906
Camp (Islafoot) | Orientation: Unknown | NX 85973 99122

The fort is located on a plain slightly above the bank of the River Nith, while on the opposite shore is the camp. Both sites have the potential to be overlooked. It seems likely that the fort (and possibly the camp) were built to secure the road north, which splits in the vicinity of the site, with one route likely to be heading into Ayrshire and the other towards central Scotland. The site was investigated as part of a *Time Team*

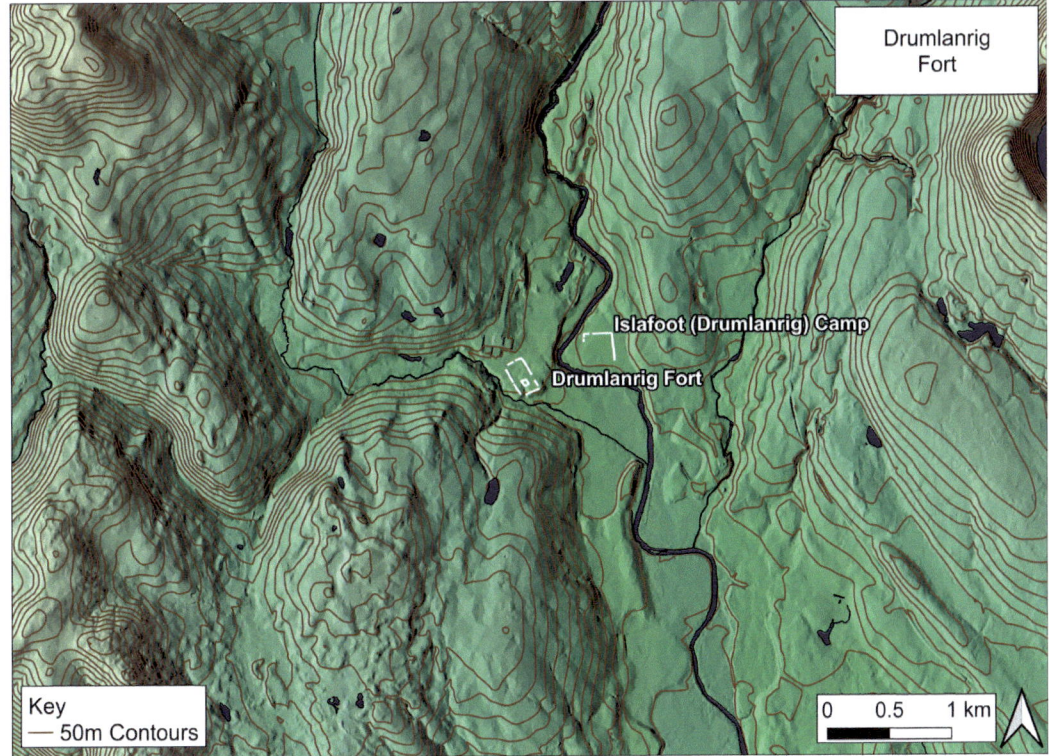

The sites at Drumlanrig.

episode, although this was limited and focussed on the fort. The *principia* was located during geophysical survey and the *Time Team* excavations, indicating the fort faces north-east. From the known defences, and a lack of detail on the interior and the entrances, it is not possible to identify the orientation of the camp. Dating of this site is difficult. When the fort was identified from the air, the ditch terminal at the southern end was of the parrot-beak style, indicating a Flavian date for the site. However, when it was surveyed and excavated for *Time Team*, the excavators found the remains of Antonine pottery and nothing that was Flavian, leading them to conclude that there was no first-century occupation phase on the fort site. However, they did note that they could not excavate the annexe and, as such, could not rule out that there may be earlier remains underneath it. The camp (one of three in the local area) is assumed to be Flavian because of its proximity to the forts.

Durisdeer
Camps | Orientation: Unknown | NS 89138 03092

Durisdeer is the location of two camps, one built inside the other. Perched at the entrance to the glens, they are most likely protecting the route towards Clydesdale and were superseded by the Antonine fortlet, which is sited further up the valley.

Remains of the second-century fortlet at Durisdeer.

The sites are to the east of the Carron Water, with the Hapland Burn to the south, while the Kirk Burn runs around the north and west. The second-century road has not been located further south than the village of Durisdeer, but it is assumed that it follows the route of the modern road across the site. If it does, then the road does not respect the boundaries of the camps, indicating that they were likely to have been constructed before the Antonine period. The square shape of the outer camp, and lack of identifiable gates, make it impossible to discern the orientation. The inner camp is more complete, but trapezoidal in shape, and has an unidentified northern gate, making it difficult to calculate the orientation. However the positioning of the southern gate implies that it may be the *porta sinistra* and that the camp faces north-east. If it faces this way it would command views of the valley, which the later road follows. Both camps are assumed to be Flavian as they share similarities with other camps of the period.

Fourmerkland
Camp | Orientation: 92° (East) | NX 91502 80052

Located on a raised platform overlooking the Cluden Water to the south, there is a small burn protecting the northern flank. Despite being overlooked to the south-west, the site has good views over most of the surrounding area. The highest point of the fort is the western gate and, along with the positioning of the entrances, indicates the camp is orientated to the east and may face an untraced section of Roman road. Discovered in 1949, the camp has not been excavated, but it is assumed to date to the first century because of similarities with other early camps.

Gatehouse of Fleet

Fortlet | Orientation: 42° (North-east) | NX 59550 57373

The fortlet, initially identified as a small fort, is located on a raised platform overlooking the Water of Fleet, making use of the natural topography for defence. The site is overlooked to the east, and is positioned to guard this section of the river. However, the banking is steep here and no crossing points have been identified, although erosion may have affected the riverbank. Aerial photographs of the site, and excavations have revealed the entrance faced north-east, away from the river. It seems likely that it was facing a road approaching the crossing, although no traces of such a route have been identified. Pottery recovered during excavation has indicated Flavian activity.

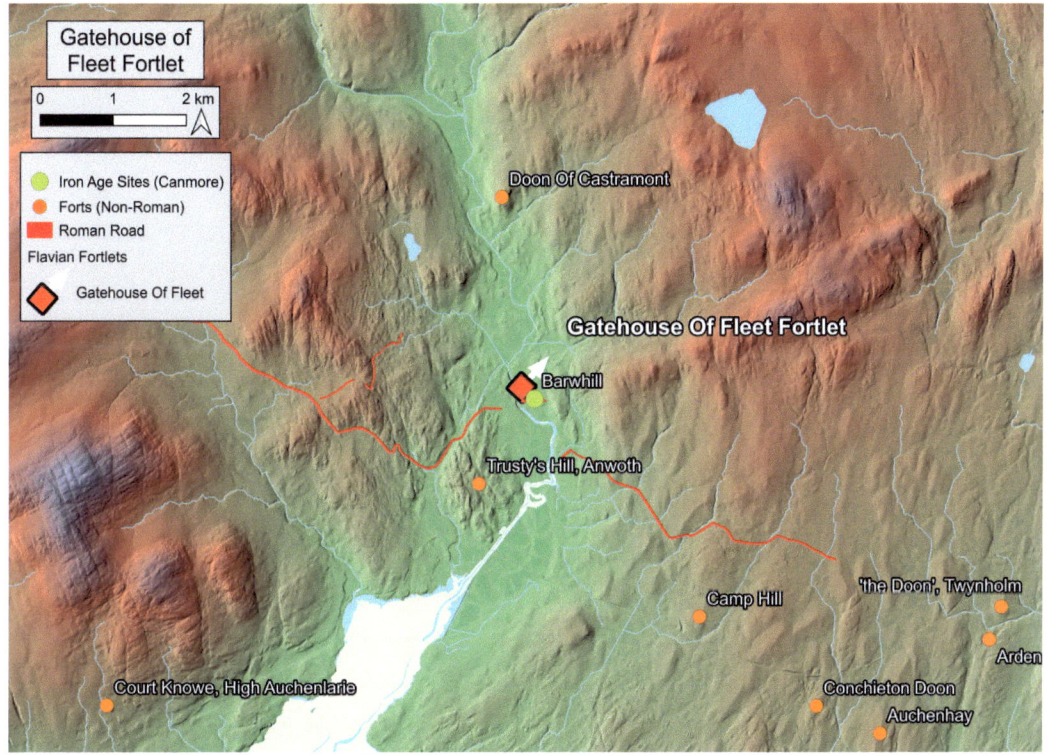

Orientation of Gatehouse of Fleet fortlet.

Glenlochar

Fort | Orientation: 263° (West) | NX 73500 64528
Camp I (Possible) | Orientation: Unknown | NX 73549 64878

The fort and at least four camps of differing periods are located on the eastern bank of the River Dee by the Glenlochar Barrage, which was constructed to create a reservoir in the early twentieth century. While this has not affected the known archaeology, it indicates that any crossing will have been lost, although a small, possibly canalised, channel runs to the north of the site and may be of some antiquity. The identification of a road heading north, as well as the east–west route and potential river crossing, indicates that Glenlochar was an important location on the transport network, and one that was guarded by the fort. Limited excavation of the site, along with aerial imagery, has led to a plan of the site, implying the fort faces south-east, towards the river and a probable crossing point. The Roman road has been located on the opposite bank. The gates of the camp have not been identified, so it is not possible to say which direction the site faces. Identified in the middle of the twentieth century, excavations of the fort indicated at least three phases of occupation: Flavian and two Antonine, and a possible second Flavian phase (based on comparisons with the 1911

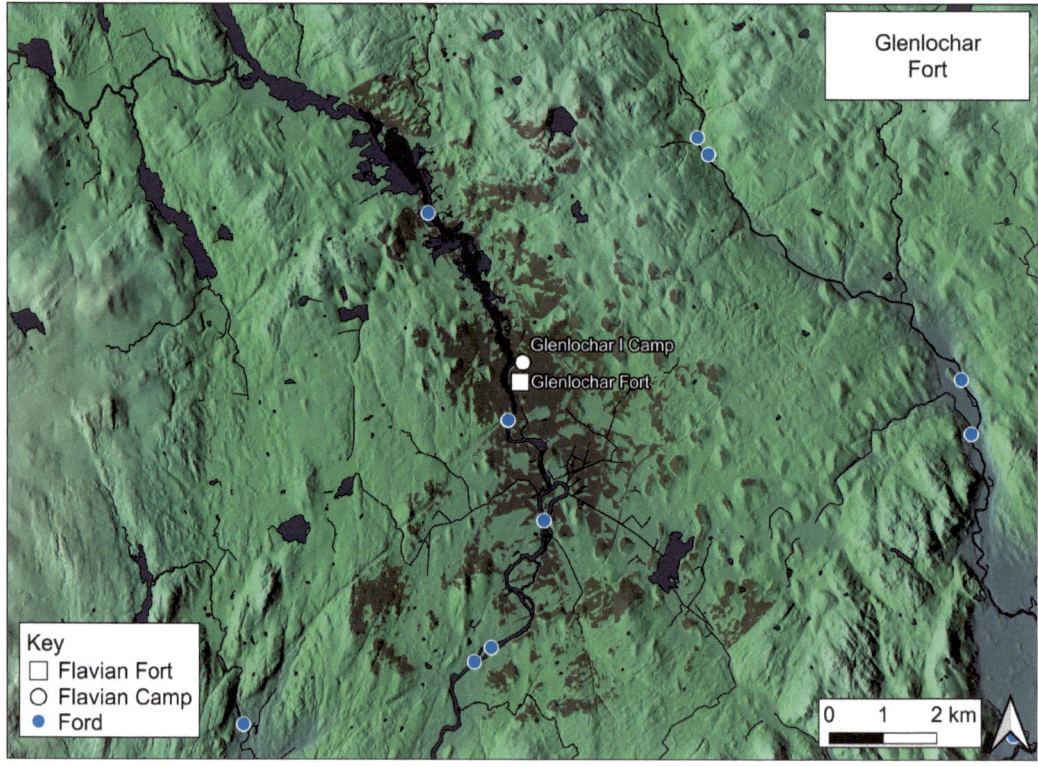

Visible area (dark shading) from Glenlochar fort.

excavations at Newstead). These dating conclusions were based on Antonine finds in the later phases of the fort, concluding that the layers below this were earlier. Only one pottery fragment was confirmed as being Flavian. Given their proximity to the fort, the camps have been ascribed similar dates.

Glenluce

Camp | Orientation: 207° (South-west) | NX 19805 56603

Positioned on a steep slope, the camp is overlooking the Water of Luce, near to where it flows into the Solway Firth. The camp at Glenluce marks the most westerly site in Dumfries and Galloway. The camp has excellent views over the Solway Firth to the west and south-west, although the views are restricted to the south and south-east. The camp is well positioned to guard the river, and the strong views over the Irish Sea suggests this was a strategically important area. The Roman road from Glenlochar to Stranraer was recorded in 1992 from the air and was noted to run to the south of the camp. No dating evidence has been found, but it is thought to date to the first century given that it is on a Roman road linking other Flavian fortifications.

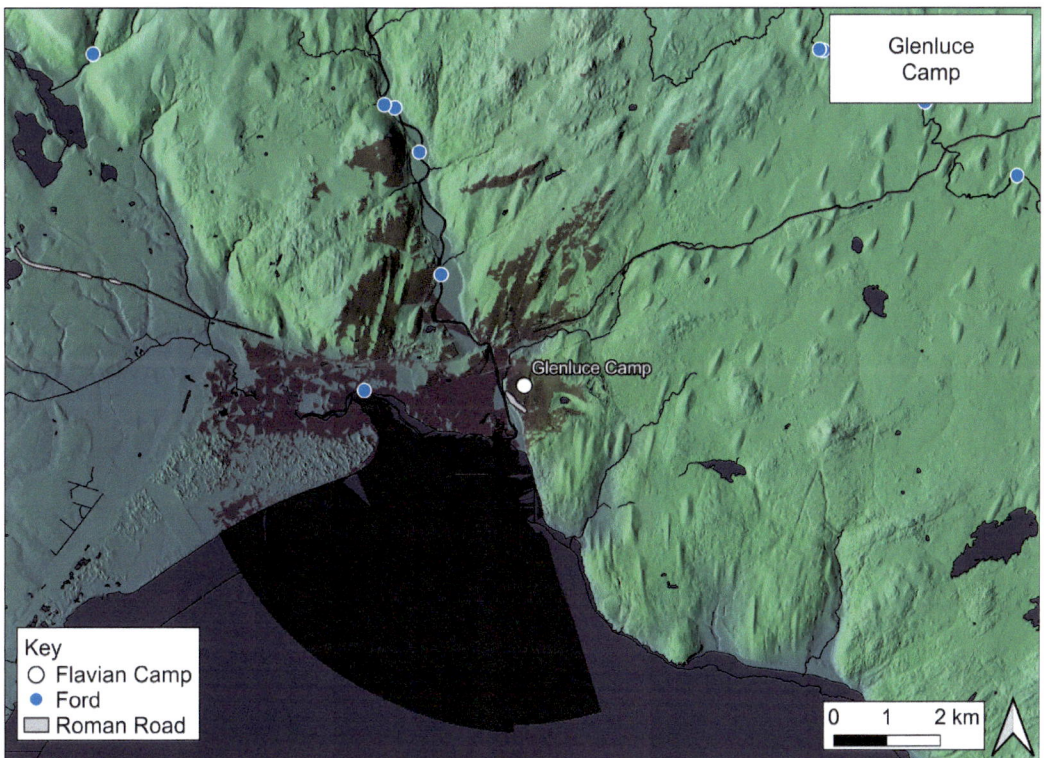

Visible area (dark shading) from Glenluce camp.

Kirkland

Fortlet | Orientation: Unknown | NX 80413 90113

Positioned on a small hill in the bottom of the river valley for the Cairn Water, the site is overlooked by hills to the south, and potentially guards a crossing point over the river. The immediate area to the south of the fortlet has been destroyed by the construction of a railway line, while the northern edge has been eroded by the waterway. Despite being excavated, it is unclear where the entrance was, although it may have been on the uncharted north-north-west side. The road, if there is one, has not been located, but any traces may have been eroded. Discovered during reconnaissance and subsequently excavated, the fortlet had one period of occupation and was then demolished. Although the datable evidence has been found at Kirkland, the excavators have postulated that it was built in the first century.

Milton

Fort | Orientation: Unknown | NT 09233 01419
Camps (Possible) | Orientation: 76° (East) | NT 09233 01419

Milton is the location of a number of Roman fortifications dating to the Antonine and Flavian periods, with some indication of Hadrianic and pre-Flavian activity. The sites are located on a hill or ridge overlooking the valley of the River Clyde to the east, and is a little to the south of the confluences of the river with the Moffat and Annan Waters. The sites have good views of the rest of the surrounding area, while the Roman road runs to the east. Not enough of the fort defences are known to identify the direction it is facing, while the long and short axis of the camp are identifiable indicating that the camp is orientated to the east. The fort was excavated in the mid-twentieth century, with excavators speculating it dates to the first century because there are broad similarities in the shape of the fort with other sites such as Bochastle and Newstead. Further work revealed a number of fragments of first-century pottery. There is also evidence of an early structure on the site, interpreted as a camp, although there are similarities with the early ditches found beneath the forts at Castledykes and Birrens. This could suggest activity at the fort that is either pre- or very early Flavian. The camp is assumed to date to the first century because part of the defences lie beneath the fort.

Raeburnfoot

Camp | Orientation: 209° (South-west) | NY 25000 99598

The camp at Raeburnfoot is located on a hillside overlooking the river valley of the White Esk, which passes by the south-eastern side of the site, and the Rae Burn to the east. The two rivers meet a little to the south (and close to the later Roman fort). There is some indication that the nearby fort has been eroded by the river, which may explain why the camp is located on higher ground. The Roman road runs to the east of the site, on a north–south alignment, with archaeologists speculating that it is heading northwards towards the Eildon Hills. The positioning of the gates indicate this camp faces south-west. Only identified in 2002, the camp has parrot-beak style gates, which indicates first-century origins.

Ward Law

Camp | Orientation: Unknown | NY 02400 66870

The camp at Ward Law is located towards the summit of a hill, forming part of the Dundonald range, with good views over the Solway Firth to the south-east, south and south-west. To the east of the site is the Lochar Water, although it flows into the Firth several miles further east. Originally, Ward Law was interpreted as a fort, and it is only in the twenty-first century that this view has been revised, and the site is now believed to be a camp. Either way, the camp is in a particularly strategic position, and may have acted as a frontier outpost for

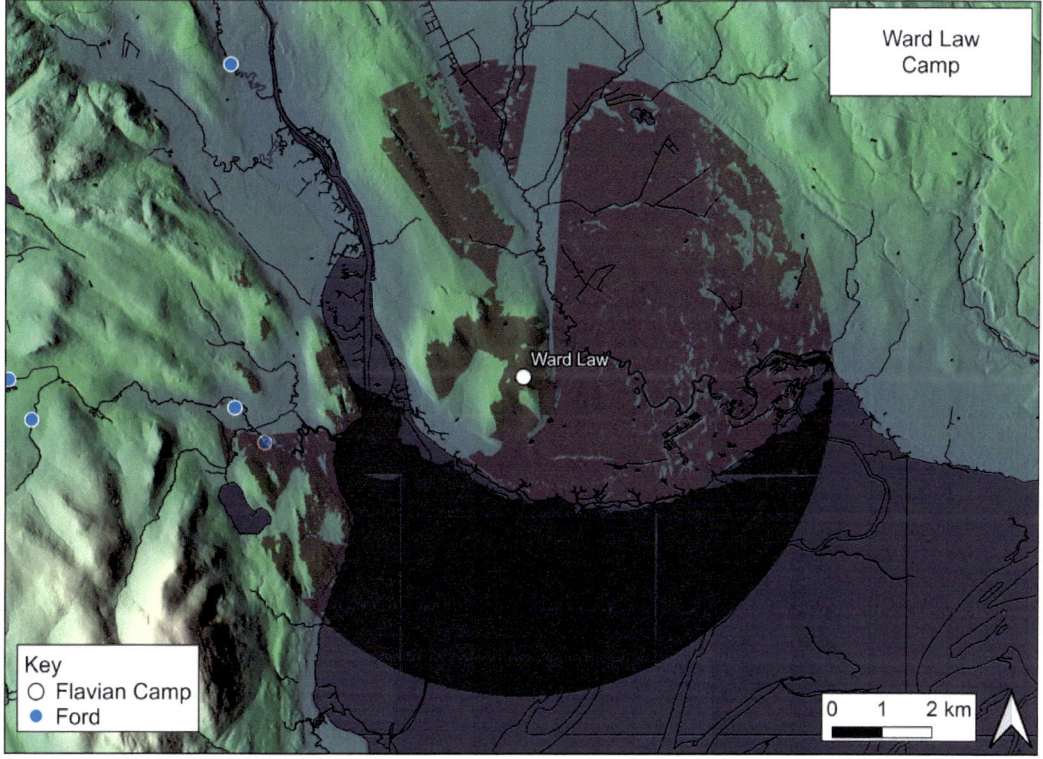

Visible area (dark shading) from Ward Law camp.

the Stanegate or Hadrian's Wall (depending on the dating). Alternatively, Ward Law may have been established as part of a chain of sites along the north side of the Solway Firth as part of the Agricolan invasion, creating or securing a route that followed the coast before heading northwards. It does seem logical to create a series of installations, securing the coastline and an east–west route; however, more datable evidence is required to confirm this conclusion. While the long axis of the camp defences has been identified, the gates on are not opposite the gates on the north-west. This may be due to the local topography, but makes it difficult to identify the orientation. A small, well-preserved indigenous fort is south of the Roman site, covering an area of 0.27 hectares, and assumed to date to the Iron Age, although no artefacts or other datable evidence has been recorded so it is unclear whether it was occupied before or after the Roman camp was established. The Roman site was excavated by St Joseph, who failed to find any datable artefacts or distinctive internal features. He noted that the western end of Hadrian's Wall could clearly be seen from the site, speculating that it may have been a Hadrianic outpost. Given the positioning of the camp on the Solway coast, and that other fortifications along the southern side of Dumfries and Galloway date to the Flavian period, it is a logical assumption that Ward Law also dates to this time. The fortlet at Lantonside (1 kilometre to the west) is close, although it is dated to the Antonine period. However, between the two sites, there is visual control of both the Solway coast and the mouth of the River Nith.

Edinburgh

Gogar Green
Camp | Orientation: Unknown | NT 1765 7175

Located on a flat plain, the camp is not overlooked, has good views of the surrounding area and is not near any major stretches of water. The Gogar Burn is to the north of the site, but the area has been heavily developed, with watercourses diverted for ornamental features. As just two sides have been identified, it is not possible to say which way it faces. Although no Roman roads have been located in the area, some suggest that Dere Street runs nearby, heading west towards the forts at Camelon. The camp was excavated in the mid-1980s, before construction of the city bypass, and is considered Flavian because of its position to the south of the western route from Edinburgh and because it is not too far from the presumed original site of the Ingliston milestone (itself undated). This supports the theory that Dere Street headed inland toward the Forth-Clyde isthmus.

Falkirk

Camelon
Fort (North) | Orientation: 67° (North-east) | NS 8630 8097
Fort (South) | Orientation: Unknown | NS 8630 8097

The double fort complex at Camelon is situated above the valley of the River Caron, taking advantage of its natural topography. The area appears to have been a central point for fortifications, with several camps in the area, including those at nearby Lochlands. The landscape has been heavily altered by industrial activity, and this includes the river valley. There has been some speculation, supported by limited circumstantial evidence, that Camelon may have been the site of a Roman harbour, and had water levels been higher, it would have been accessible from the Firth of Forth. The North Fort appears to be facing downriver, providing it with good views of any approaching river traffic. It is likely that the forts were built here to guard a crossing, or a harbour. The excavations of the North Fort revealed the layout of the *principia*, indicating the orientation of the site to the north-east. The South Fort has been extensively developed

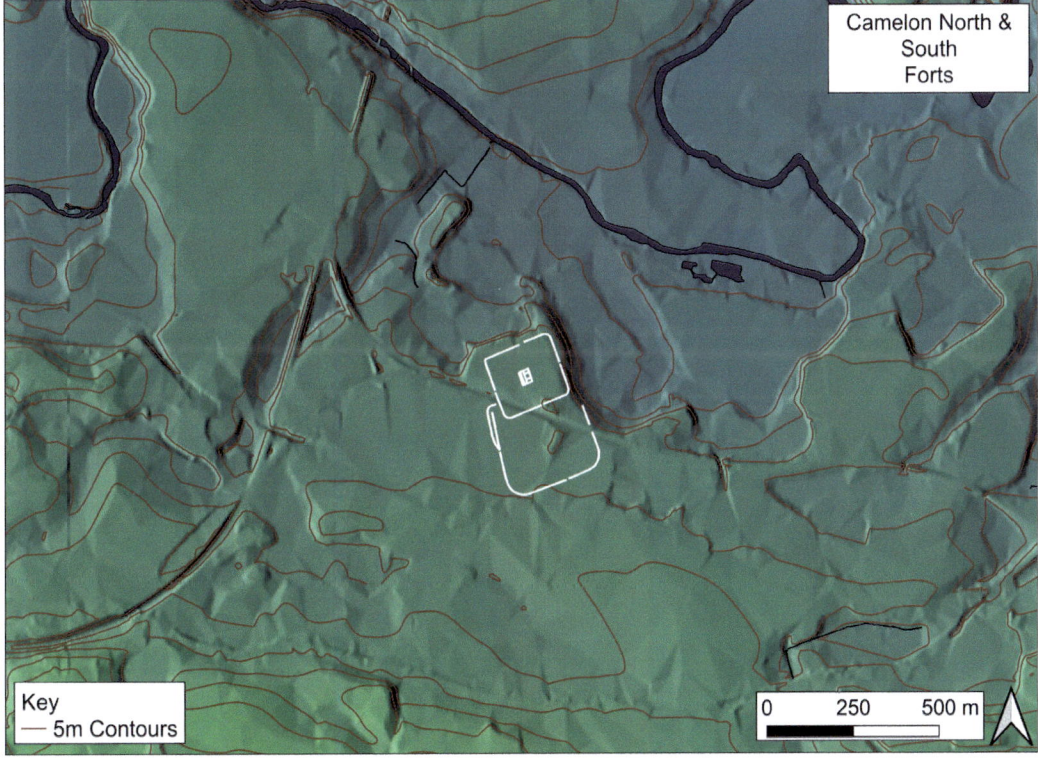

The forts at Camelon.

over the past couple of hundred years, limiting any possibility of discerning the direction it faces, although from the positioning of the gates it could face either north-east or north-west. The earliest excavations were undertaken at the beginning of the twentieth century when the sites were distinguished as the North and South forts. Pottery from the North site indicated a Flavian date for that part of the site. While there have been numerous finds from the South Fort, Flavian activity at the site was not confirmed until the 1970s.

Lochlands
Camps II, IV, VI | Orientation: Unknown | NS 8530 8160

Located on a spur in the River Caron, which runs around the north-eastern, northern and north-western sides of the fortifications, there are a number of potential encampments here. Lochlands is also in close proximity to the forts at Camelon. The camps may have protected a major route northward, and possibly a crossing point over the river, and seems to have been a gathering point for the army. The location is postulated as a place where soldiers practised building camps. The local area has subsequently been heavily developed. It is not clear which camp came first, or when they were constructed. Not enough of the defences of any of the camps have been located to indicate which way they face. There are indications that the earliest fortifications predated the adjacent Roman road, which suggests that they were positioned on early routes. The road runs from the south-east to the north-west, crossing the Caron at an unknown point, and cuts through camp III and IV, implying that some camps predate the road, and then abandoned by the time the later fortifications were constructed. Dating the various camps has proven complicated because they overlap and, in some instances, only parts of the defences have been identified. Camp IV has yielded pottery indicating a Flavian date, while there is speculation that camp VI is the earliest known fortification on the site.

Lanarkshire

Carnwath
Camp (Bankhead II) | Orientation: Unknown | NS 98288 45008
Fortlet | Orientation: Unknown | NS 98288 45008

Located overlooking the river valley, where the Medwin Water meets the River Clyde, there are two camps (one Flavian) and a fortlet in the immediate area. Both sites were overlooked by the sides of the river valley. The fortlet, partly destroyed by quarrying, is immediately north of the current course of the River Clyde, although it is located by a loop in the river, which would not have been suitable for crossing. The Roman road runs to the north of the site. The topography on the opposite bank does not lend itself to a road. Given the route of the known section of Roman road, it was constructed after camp II was built and abandoned. The camp is square, so it is not possible to identify any of the features that would indicate which way it faces. Despite a limited excavation of the fortlet, the excavators could not locate the entrance because of ploughing and the construction of the railway through the site, but they speculated it lay on the north side. This suggests that the fortlet is potentially facing the road, which would mean that it was constructed at the same time or after it was laid down, and therefore later than camp II. Camp II has a *tituli* on the northern sides, suggesting a first-century date. Like several of the camps in southern Scotland, the Roman road appears to bisect the site, indicating that it may be later than the camp, as it is not respecting its boundaries (which it does for camp I). It's possible that camp II predates both camp I and the road. Some suggest that camp II could result from realignment of camp I to fit in with the road. The fortlet is assumed to be Flavian because of its dimensions and triple ditch arrangement, which is similar to the fortlet at Castle Greg (West Lothian), which can be dated to the first century.

Castledykes
Fort | Orientation: 192° (South) | NS 92864 44258
Camps IA and B | Orientation: Unknown | NS 92272 44765
Camp IV | Orientation: Unknown | NS 931 445

The fort and the camps are between the River Clyde, to the south, and the Mouse Water, a little to the north. There are several fortifications from different periods here, with the Roman road passing to the south of the camps, possibly indicating that they were constructed at the same time as the route, or once its path had been planned. The known road is on an east–west trajectory, passing through the gates of the Antonine fort. The Flavian fort appears to predate the road in this area, as the known route respects the boundaries of the Antonine fort, breaching those of the earlier Flavian installation. Although parts of the camp defences are known, they respect the line of the road, which could suggest the Flavian fort was constructed first, then the road or the camps came almost at the same time. Excavation has shown the first-century fort faces south, towards the River Clyde, although there is no known crossing point here. Not enough remains of the camps have been identified to indicate the direction they face. Known since the eighteenth century, the fort wasn't excavated until almost 200 years later. During work beneath the rampart of the Antonine fort, first-century pottery and a coin were recovered, indicating first-century activity. At least four camps have been identified around the fort, with camp IA assumed to be Flavian because of the parrot-beak style entrances. It is not clear when IA was reduced to form IB. Dating of the sites is complex due to the discovery of partial outlines of the defences and because the camps overlap in places. Some archaeologists have suggested that camp IV is Flavian, as it overlaps with the fort.

Cold Chapel
Camp | Orientation: Unknown | NS 9352 2490

Little is known about the camp at Cold Chapel, except that it is located on the main western Roman road towards central Scotland from Carlisle, following a line of fortifications up the Clyde river valley. While the camp is located next to the River Clyde, there is no indication of a crossing and, given the position of the next site further north, the camp at Wandel, which is on the right-hand bank of the river, it seems unlikely that there would have been a crossing at this point. Not enough of the defences have been identified to calculate the orientation, although it seems likely that it faced north-east or south-west. Archaeologists have suggested that it is a Flavian site, belonging to a group of camps (Cornhill–Carlops) thought to be an early first-century chain of sites from the earliest Roman incursion into Scotland.

Cornhill
Camp | Orientation: 214° (South-west) | NT 0215 3574

The camp at Cornhill is located on a hillside, to the east of the River Clyde, and would have been overlooked. The site was first photographed in 1949, but not fully identified as a camp until 1976. The Roman road runs to the south-east of the site, on the other side of a hill from the camp, but may not have been visible from parts of the fortification. The camp does not appear to be facing the road or a river crossing. The long and short axis of the camp are identifiable, indicating that the camp faced south-west. The camp forms part of the Cornhill–Carlops chain of camps attributed to the early Flavian period.

Crawford
Fort | Orientation: 144° (South-east) | NS 9538 2143

The fort sits in a wide stretch of the Clyde valley, with the river running a little way to the south. It is overlooked to the south and north. The fort is unusual because it does not follow the rules followed by most other forts – that the *principia* should be opposite one of the short axis. Instead, Crawford is a rectangular fort with the *principia* looking out of the long axis, a feature that is shared with Loudoun Hill and some Antonine forts (e.g. Rough Castle and Bearsden), indicating the fort faces south-east, to the junction of Roman roads from Annandale and Nithsdale.

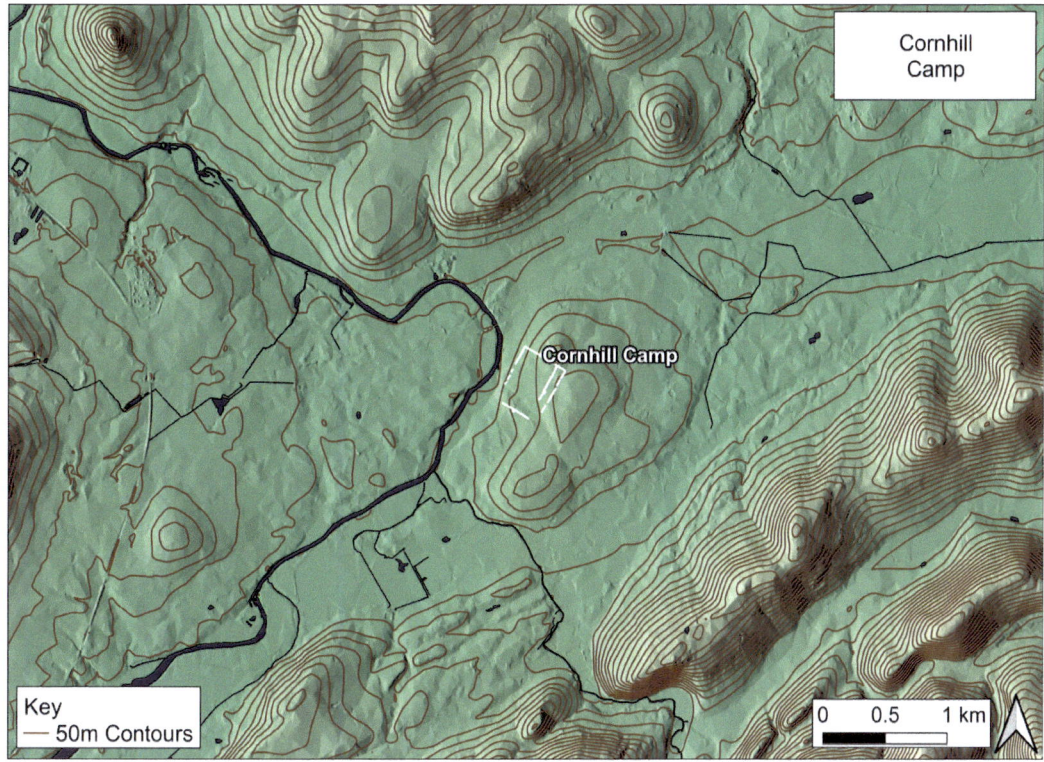

The camp at Cornhill.

Therefore, the fort may have been guarding the crossing point over the River Clyde. There was an eighteenth-century rumour of a Roman site at Crawford, which wasn't confirmed until excavation in the late 1930s. A larger-scale series of excavations were undertaken from 1961 to 1966, which revealed three phases of occupation, including one from the Flavian period. A single fragment of pottery gave a first-century occupation date for the site.

Kirkhouse
Camp | Orientation: 125° (South-east) | NT 0980 4620

The fort is located on a slope towards the bottom of a valley, and overlooked by the hills to the north-west and west. The Roman road runs south-west to the north-east and crosses over part of the site, indicating that Dere Street was constructed after the camp was abandoned. Although the south-eastern defences have not yet been located, there are gaps on the north-eastern and south-western sides, which may have been gates. While no datable artefacts were uncovered during excavation, it is assumed to date to the Flavian period because of its relationship with the road.

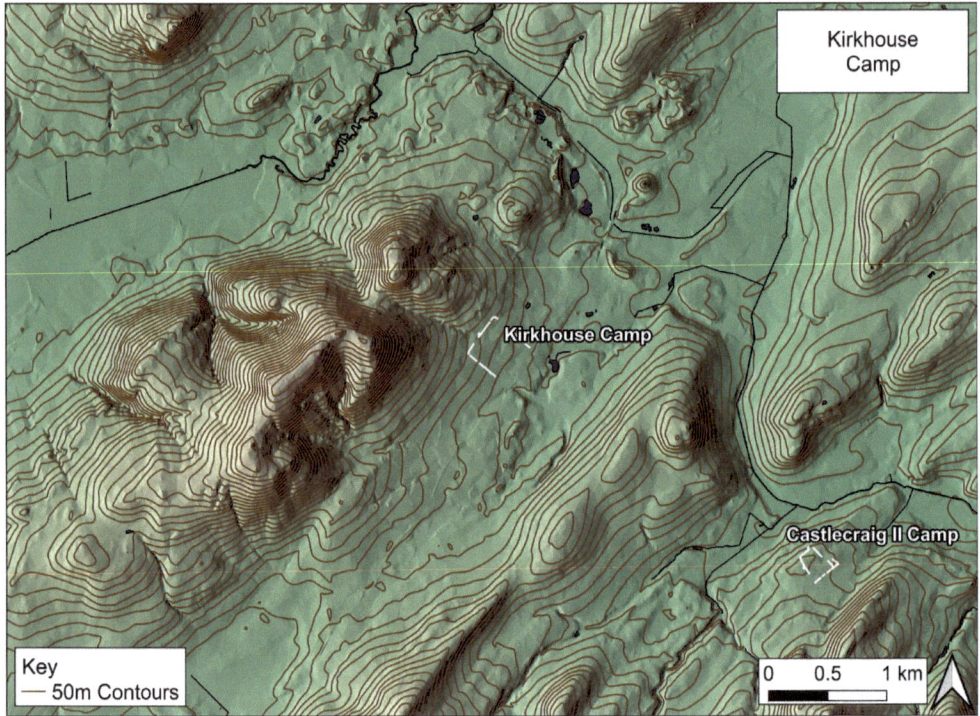

The camp at Kirkhouse.

Lamington

Camp | Orientation: Unknown | NS 977 309

The camp overlooks the valley where the River Clyde flows, and is 50 metres from an undated Roman fortlet (NS 977 307), which appears to be guarding the adjacent road. The site would have been overlooked from most sides, but particularly the south and south-east. The Lamington Burn flows to the north and into the River Clyde nearby. Not enough of the defences have been located to identify the orientation. The road is suspected of running to the south-east of the site, underneath the modern A702. This seems likely given that the fortlet is next to the road and likely to be contemporary with it, although as no excavations have taken place on the camp, fortlet, or road. It is not possible to say what relationship these had with each other. Maybe the camp was located here to guard a route before the road was constructed, and the fortification being superseded by the fortlet. There are two fords nearby, which are marked on older Ordnance Survey maps: Haddington Mains to the north-west of the camp, which is suspected of being of recent origin; and Hartside, which has existed since at least the 1860s, although has since been lost in places due to fluvial movements. The camp is undated, but is presumed to be Flavian because of similarities it shares with other similar-sized sites elsewhere in Scotland.

Mollins

Fort | Orientation: Unknown | NS 7139 7189

Located by a river valley (the Luggie Water) to the north of Mollins fort, the course has been altered by construction works over the years. The fort is in a good position to look up and down the valley, but the landscape has been significantly altered through industrial activity, as well as construction of the adjacent motorway network. The purpose of the fort at this location is not clear, especially as no Roman roads have been identified nearby. There has been a suggestion that the nearby modern crossing at My Lords Bridge may be much older, with the implication being that the fort was guarding a Roman crossing point over the Luggie Water. The full defences of the fort have not been identified so it is not possible to determine the direction it faced. The site was excavated towards the end of the 1970s, with limited pottery recovered. One fragment – from the soil that had gathered in the ditch after the site was abandoned – was dated to AD 60–90, so the dating for this site is by no means conclusive.

Wandel

Camp | Orientation: Unknown | NS 944 267

The camp at Wandel is located towards the bottom of the Clyde river valley, and is overlooked by Wandel Hill to the south-east, and there is an adjacent Antonine fortlet. The Roman road, which heads north, runs to the east of the camp and parallel with the river. The camp (and later fortlet) may have been located here to protect the road as there is no indication of a river crossing close by, although there are a couple of possible sites and sections of road to the west. No datable finds were recovered during excavation, but given its positioning alongside the Roman road it seems probable that the camp is contemporary with this and potentially dates to the Flavian invasion of Scotland.

Midlothian

Elginhaugh

Fort | Orientation: 186° (South) | NT 32134 67346

Standing on a headland, created by river erosion, the square fort of Elginhaugh is on the north bank of the River North Esk, making use of the steepness of the river valley to protect the south side of the site. Running east–west through the site is Dere Street, which is then believed to follow the line of the A68 and the A7. The fort may have been built in this location to protect a nearby river crossing, and the landscape at this point does not suggest that a ford was in use. The site has been extensively excavated, revealing that the

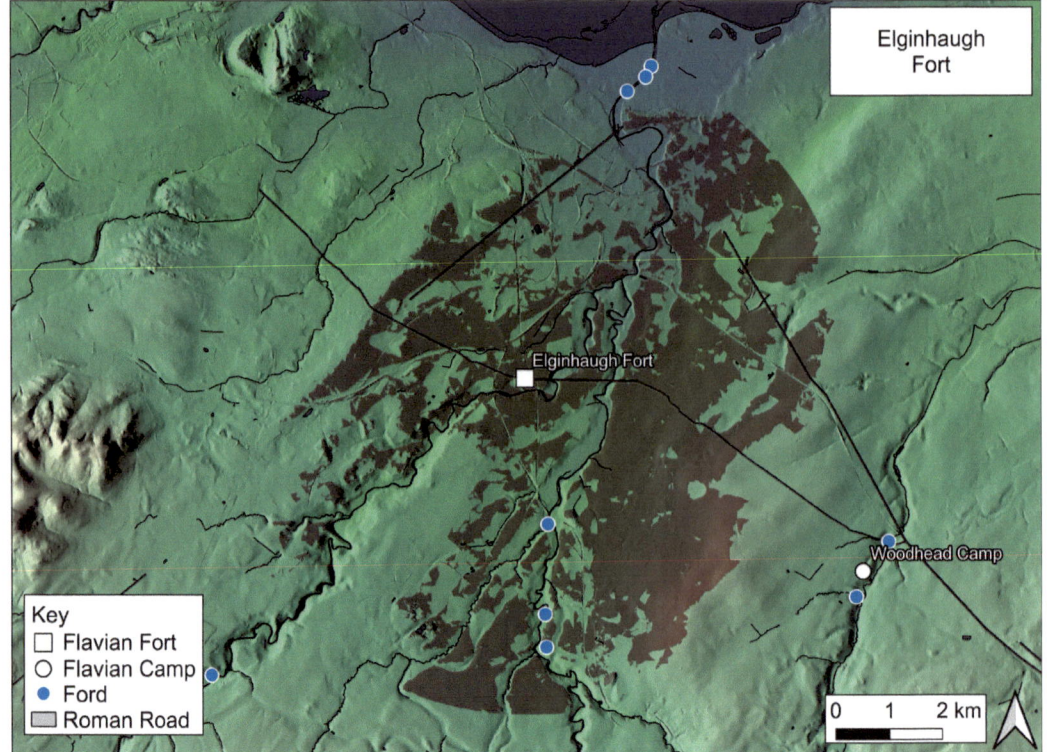

Visible area (dark shading) from Elginhaugh fort.

fort was orientated south. The main gate faces into an annexe, beyond which is the more recent Elginhaugh Bridge (NT 3214 6710), which crosses the North Esk. Identified in 1979, the Roman fort had been photographed a few years previously but went unrecognised. It was subsequently excavated to confirm its Roman origins, with a fragment of Samian pottery recovered that was dated to before AD 90. Before development on the site it was extensively excavated. A coin hoard was recovered from a construction trench of the *principia,* indicating that the headquarters could not have been built any later than AD 78.

Carlops Spittal
Camp | Orientation: Unknown | NT 1715 5725

The camp at Carlops Spittal is located on a ridge that runs parallel with the adjacent hill, with the site taking advantage of the natural topography. The River North Esk runs to the east of the site, although it is not a substantial waterway. Several streams run into the river near the site of the camp, and it is likely that these were much more substantial in previous years as the construction of the North Esk Reservoir to the north-west restricted water flow in the area. Built alongside Dere Street, the road passes through the defences of the site, indicating

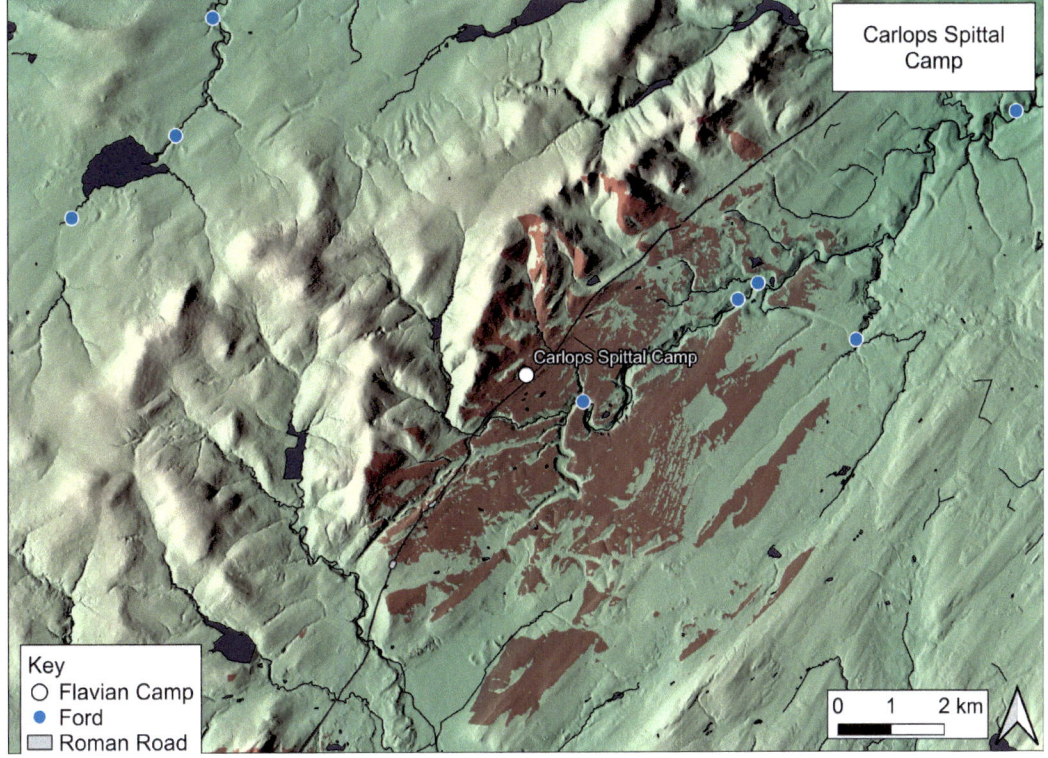

Visible area (dark shading) from Carlops Spittal camp.

that it is later than the camp. The north-eastern side of the camp is facing the route that the road takes, although it is most likely following the natural topography. The precise orientation of the site is unknown, although it is either north-east or south-west. Carlops has been grouped together with several other camps, forming a chain running from the Upper Clyde valley to the Pentlands, and are argued to predate Dere Street as the road cuts across the defences of several sites (Carlops, Kirkhouse and Wandel). No datable evidence has come from this site, but as it is earlier than Dere Street it seems likely to date to the Flavian period.

Woodhead
Camp I | Orientation: 214° (South-west) | NT 38411 63867
Camp II | Orientation: Unknown | NT 384 639

Located above the valley of the Tyne Water, the camps are on a hillside but also slightly overlooked by higher ground to the south-east. The positioning next to the river valley, which is accessible by a steep descent on both sides (by at least 50 metres in a short space), would have added an additional layer of defence. The Tyne Water is to the east of the camp, while slightly further to the south is the Vogrie Burn. The purpose of these camps is not clear; they do not appear to be guarding a route or crossing over the river, leading to speculation by some that Woodhead played the role of a timber yard for construction at Elginhaugh. However, this is not a particularly convincing argument, given that it would appear to be the only example of such a site, and 7 kilometres is a long distance to transport large tree trunks used in building the fort. Environmental analysis of timbers from Elginhaugh, and of the landscape in and around the camps, would help to rule out such a possibility. To the north of the site is Dere Street, which seemingly splits just before Woodhead. The positioning of the gates of camp I indicate this camp faces south-west, while the peculiar shape of camp II does suggest the direction it is likely to face. It is interesting to note that there are a number of indigenous forts in the hills surrounding the camps, and the multiple sides of camp II may be a response to this. The two camps, one seemingly inside the other, were originally identified from the air in 1976, and excavated in 1983. No datable artefacts were recovered during the excavation, and the site is the only camp on Dere Street with parrot-beak style gates, so is assumed to date to the first century.

Moray

Auchinhove
Camp | Orientation: 207° (South-west) | NJ 46185 51705

The camp is located on a gentle rise in the valley of the River Isla, on the north bank. There are hills to the north and south overlooking the site. It is particularly close to the camps at Muiryfold and Burnfield (see Aberdeenshire, p. 26), which were occupied during the Flavian period. Only the east side of this camp survives relatively complete. The west and south sides are partially known, and the north is lost under the modern road. It is not possible to say with certainty in which direction

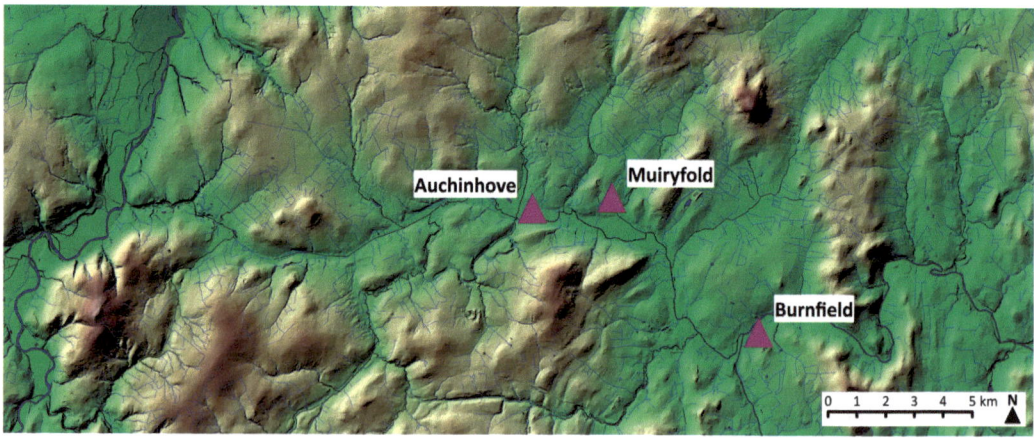

Roman camps in Moray.

the camp faced, although the highest point of the site is on the north side, which may have been the *porta decumana*, implying the camp may face south, towards the River Isla. Auchinhove has a parrot-beak type gate, indicating it is a first-century site.

Bellie
Camp (Crawford) | Orientation: Unknown | NJ 3572 6158
Camp (St Joseph) | Orientation: Unknown | NJ 3550 6109
Camp (Aerial Photograph) | Orientation: Unknown | NJ 3581 6167

The sites sit to the east of the River Spey and are a short distance from where it flows into the Moray Firth. They appear to have been located on a slight rise, just above the river flood plain. There are three possible sites for the camp at Bellie: one identified by Crawford, another by St Joseph, and a third area identified from aerial photographs by Rebecca Jones in *Roman Camps in Scotland*. While the remains were recorded as early as 1799, the specific location has not been satisfactorily confirmed. Twentieth-century investigations by Crawford, St Joseph and Daniels occurred in different places, while Jones came up with a third possible site after re-examining aerial photographs of the area. No Roman roads have been identified in the area, although there are several fords across the River Spey that have been marked on older Ordnance Survey maps. Only partial defences of each site have been recorded, therefore it is not possible to discern the orientation of the potential camps. No datable evidence of Roman activity has been recovered from the site, but as the only other Roman sites in the area date to the Flavian period, this is the most likely period of activity at Bellie.

The case for Bellie having Roman origins remains unconfirmed, as no artefacts have been found here, and only fragmentary sections of alleged camp defences have been recorded. There is, however, an alternative non-Roman explanation for the remains identified at Bellie. During the 1746 Jacobite uprising, the river was crossed by both the Jacobite army and the British army, led by the Duke of Cumberland, though at different times. Indeed, a ford crosses the Spey close to the two southernmost camps, known as Cumberland's Crossing (NJ 343 608), appearing on both the 1872 County Series Map and in the Ordnance Survey Name Book for Banffshire. In the latter, the belief that the ford was used as the crossing point by the Duke of Cumberland in his pursuit of Bonnie Prince Charlie is recorded. It is noted that the prince instructed Lord John, part of the Jacobite forces, to ...

> ... throw up entrenchments along the banks of the Spey and to dispute the passage of that river with the Duke of Cumberland. Relying on the resistance of Lord John, who, he [Bonnie Prince Charlie] supposed would have every recourse to every possible device to defend the ford and who, if he could not

render it altogether impassable, would at least, by fortifying it with strong entrenchments, retard the approach of the Duke ...

The Chevalier de Johnstone, 1958:117

In addition, there are accounts that the government forces were camped on the western bank of the Spey, and may have entrenched their encampments for additional security. A post-Roman date for these trenches is strengthened by the only datable finds recovered from the site. During St Joseph's excavation he found a number of bottle fragments from the ditch silt, which dated to 1770–80, which he said indicated that the ditches were still uncovered around that time. The Jacobite uprising took place thirty years before these fragments were deposited. It therefore seems prudent to bear this in mind when considering whether or not Bellie is a Roman camp.

Muiryfold

Camp | Orientation: Unknown | NJ 48900 52080

Constructed on a slope and next to a burn, this camp commands some good views to the north-east and south-west. Views to the north-west are blocked by the summit

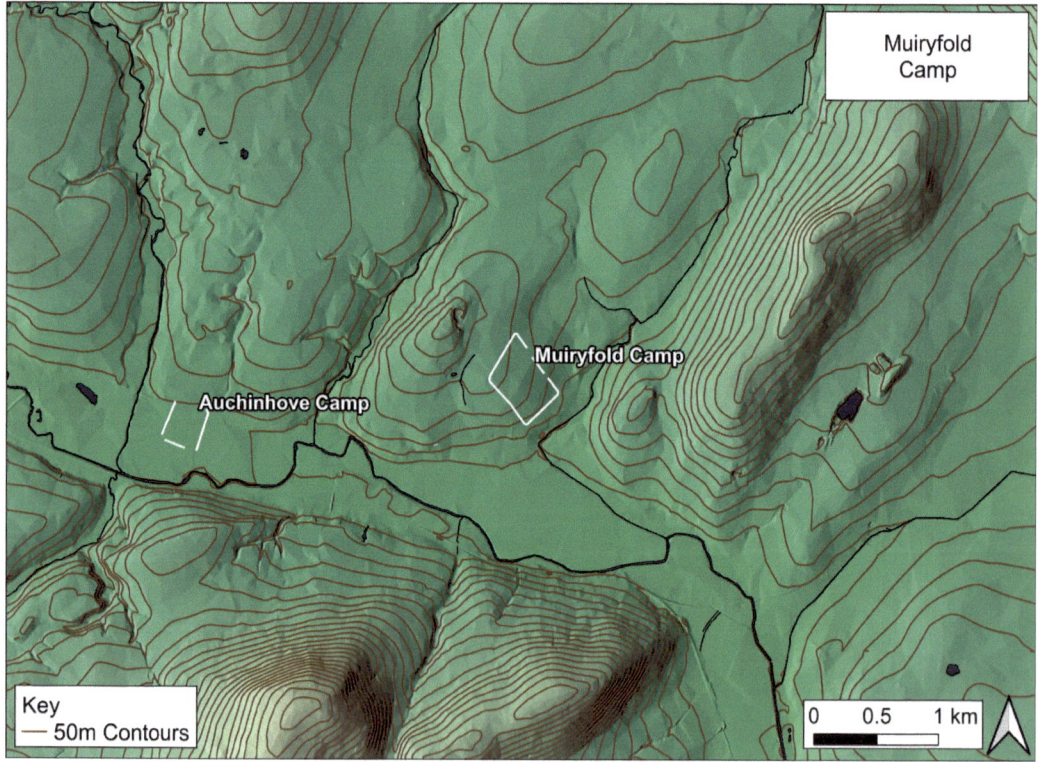

The Roman camps at Auchinhove and Muiryfold.

of the hill on which the site is located and rises to 176 metres; the camp is around 115 metres at its lowest and 145 metres at the highest. It is only 1.85 Roman miles from the camp at Auchinhove, although there are no known Roman roads nearby. Almost playing card shaped, Muiryfold faces either north-west or south-east. This site is presumed to date to the first century based on its location and the *tituli*, which have been discovered on the southern and western sides of the defences.

Perth and Kinross

Abernethy (Carey)
Camp | Orientation: Unknown | NO 17319 16458

Situated above the Tay, the camp is located on a relatively flat plain and sits in the shadow of the Ochil Hills to the south, although these are too distant to have been a risk to the site. The camp is to the immediate south of a bend in River Earn, just over a kilometre from its confluence with the Firth of Tay. The Carey Stank, which has been canalised, now flows through the site. The site commands good views out towards the Firth of Tay to the north-east and north-west. Abernethy may have faced the hill fort at Castle Law (NO 1830 1533) to the south-east, itself part of a series of indigenous fortifications noted as being occupied from 60 BC up to the Flavian period. This small oval indigenous hill fort makes use of the natural topography of the site's positioning at the tip of the outcrop at the top of Castle Law, which was excavated in the late 1898s. The excavators uncovered a defensive wall constructed from timber, which surrounds an area of 0.06 hectares. Several finds were made during the excavations (e.g. animal bones, coarse pottery, jet ring), all of which supports a pre-Roman occupation date. The Roman camp is rhomboid

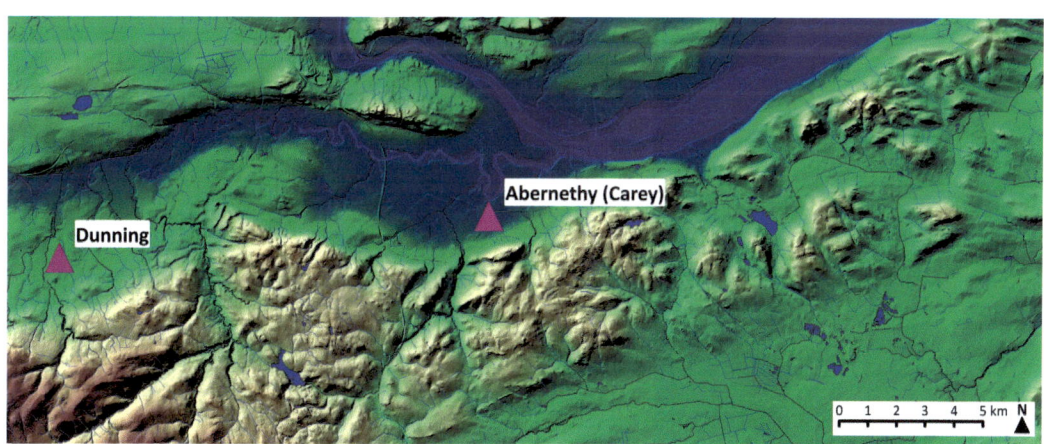

The Roman camps at Dunning and Abernethy.

shaped and has two clear gates on the south-east side and has indicative gaps on the other sides. Due to the shape, it is not possible to speculate on the orientation. The camp has claviculae in front of several entrances, indicating a first-century date. This is supported by a fragment of South Gaulish Samian pottery, which has been dated to the late first century. The site is often compared (by size and morphology) with Dunning camp and assumed to be of the same period.

Ardoch

Fort | Orientation: 185° (South) | NN 8390 0990
Camp II | Orientation: Unknown | NN 8390 1090
Camp V | Orientation: Unknown | NN 84046 10229

Known since at least the eighteenth century and first excavated at the end of that period, Ardoch is an extremely well-preserved site, surrounded by at least seven camps. There are at least two forts here, and possibly a third. The surrounding area is fairly gentle, and the sites makes use of the adjacent valley of the River Knaick. Only camp II is overlooked to the north by gentle hills, along the route of the road. The Roman road runs from the south, passing by the fort before heading north on to the Gask Ridge, and seems to cross the Allan Water and the Knaick to the south of the site. Early excavation of the fort established the

Ardoch fort.

location of the *principia*, although the dating of the building is unclear. Early plans of the fort, particularly by General Roy, appear to position the left and right gates (the *porta dextra* and the *porta sinistra*) towards the southern end of the fort, which indicates it faces south. The fort appears to have only been reduced in size when occupied and not reconstructed or reorientated. It is probable this fort has always faced south. Without extensive archaeological exploration of all the camps at Ardoch it is extremely difficult to identify the possible directions these face. It appears Ardoch II and V are both orientated north-east or south-east as they are traditional 'playing card' shaped, although less of the defences of the latter site have been identified. The earliest fort is Flavian, with dating evidence from pottery finds excavated in 1898, although the fort has been reduced in size at some point and then reoccupied in the Antonine period. There is no archaeological evidence to conclusively date camp I, but it is postulated to be Antonine due to the size. Camp II and V are earlier than camp I (likely to be post-Flavian), while camp III and IV are likely to predate camps I and II. Due to the complexity of the sites, overlaying each other, any artefacts that could provide datable evidence will need to be treated with caution when applying to each camp.

Bertha

Fort | Orientation: 44° (North-east) | NO 0974 2680

Bertha is located on low-lying, level ground by the confluence of the Almond and the Tay. It most likely guards a crossing over one, if not both, rivers, and may have been prone to flooding. The fort is likely to be facing a crossing over the Tay. The Roman road runs from the south-west, heading towards an unidentified crossing point over the waterway. A number of early antiquarian accounts mention a bridge across the Tay, while the *Old Statistical Account* details the discovery of foundations of a wooden structure which were visible at an unidentified part of the river. Subsequent attempts to locate these pillars and the bridge by a local sub-aqua team were unsuccessful. On some early maps, Derders ford (NO 10058 26865), adjacent to the confluence of the Almond, is recorded as a crossing. The site is recorded in the *Ordnance Survey Name Book for Perthshire* (1862), which claims there is a local tradition of the Romans using the ford. However, it has been suggested that it is more likely to be a weir or fish trap rather than a ford. An early plan of the defences of the fort, produced in 1919, shows that due to the positioning of the southern gate, the site faces north-east, an assertion strengthened by a geophysical survey undertaken at Bertha early in the twenty-first century. Finds recovered from the fort site during field walking in the 1970s have indicated both a Flavian and Antonine presence at the site. Prior to this a Flavian dish had also been recovered from the site.

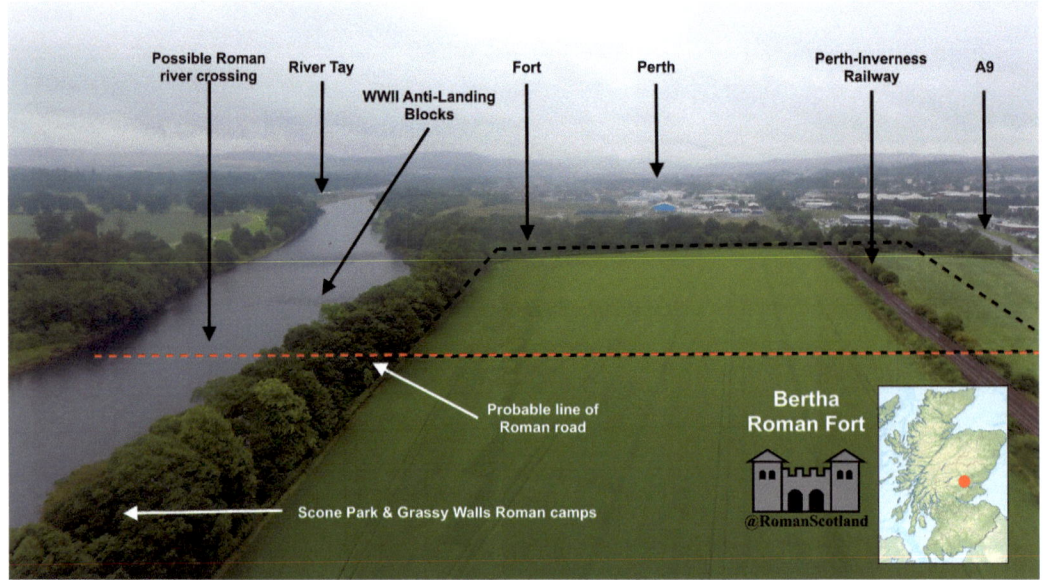

The layout of the Roman landscape by Bertha Roman fort.

Cargill
Fort | Orientation: 311° (North-west) | NO 1661 3790
Fortlet | Orientation: 325° (North-west) | NO 16347 37665

The fort is constructed on a hillside near the confluence of the Isla (which lies immediately to the north) and the Tay, and is overlooked by a hill to the south, which may have been close enough to put the interior of the fort at risk of attack. The fortlet is in a similar position. It is not clear if there is a crossing over the water in the vicinity, although this would make sense given the positioning of the fortifications. No Roman roads have been traced nearby, with the main route through the area some 2 kilometres south, and heading south-west/north-east. It does not appear to branch off to the Cargill sites, or towards the fortress at Inchtuthil. With good views in most directions, the fort would have been visible to soldiers stationed at Inchtuthil legionary fortress. Aerial survey has shown the *via principalis* of the fort, indicating it faces north-west into the annexe, which itself is bordered by the Isla. The north-east and south-west gates of the fortlet have been identified in the centre of the long axis, and as no internal features have been identified from the air or from the trial trenching, it is not possible to be more specific about the orientation. The fort has a parrot-beak-type gate, and is assumed to be Flavian. Artefacts found during excavation indicated the site was abandoned around 85 AD, a date reflected in coin finds from field walking. The fortlet has been excavated, although the results have never fully published, but the site was assumed to be Flavian. This was not confirmed until recent field walking of the site led to the discovery of shards of late first-century glass.

Dalginross

Forts | Orientation: 233° (South-west) | NN 7732 2104
Camp I | Orientation: 73° (East) | NN 7742 2078

At Dalginross there are two forts, with a smaller one sitting inside the defences of the larger one, suggesting the larger fort is older and was reduced in size to form the smaller site at a later date. The forts and camp are located on a level plain, with low-level hills to the south-east. The topography is not particularly defensive, although it is next to the river on the north-west side of the site. The sites are next to a group of at least four undated cairns or barrows (Cultybraggan), and the forts may face towards an indigenous hill fort, Mailermore (NN 752 185). This is an oval-shaped indigenous fort with a small internal area of 0.13 hectares and surrounded by a single rampart, and makes use of the defensive natural topography of a sharp drop on both the north and south sides. The site was investigated in the 1990s, and it was speculated that as the site was located at the entrance to Glen Artney, it would have performed a 'glen-blocking' function, controlling traffic moving through the valley. Aerial photography, which has revealed many internal features of the forts, indicates the *via principalis* runs along the long axis rather than the short as is more usual. Further exploration is needed to confirm this arrangement. The aerial imagery indicates the smaller fort faces south-west. No internal features for the larger fort site have been identified, so the orientation is unknown. However, the positioning of a gate a third of the way along the north-west side implies the fort is orientated south-west. Three sides of the camp exist (north-west, south-west and south-east) with a partial indication of the gate on the north-east side. The north-west and south-east gates are located three-quarters of the way along their respective sides, and although the fort is not a typical playing card shape and appears to be squarer, it is possible to speculate the camp faced east. Field walking finds collected by the Cumbernauld Historical Society in the 1970s indicate the fort and camp were occupied during both the Flavian and Antonine periods, but as one fort sits within the other it is difficult to discern which was built first. The camp has parrot-beak entrances, indicating it is Flavian.

Dunning

Camp | Orientation: Unknown | NO 02508 15025

The camp is on a hillside ranging from about 55 metre high around the ramparts to a height of around 65 metres towards the centre. The true extent of the southern boundary is unknown, and the site is overlooked to the south-east. The Dunrub Burn runs to the north of the camp, to the north-east is the Nethergarvock Burn, and to the immediate east of the camp is the Dunning Burn. Most of the south-east corner of the camp is postulated, but the positioning of gates, one in the western side and another in the south, along with two possible entrance gaps in the northern defences, could indicate the camp faced west. Despite a lack of datable evidence, the camp is assumed to date to the first century as it is a similar size and shape to the nearby camp at Abernethy. However, during excavation, ceramic remains were recovered that dated to the mid-second century. The excavators have speculated that either the camp is Antonine in date or the site was reoccupied in the later period, having originally been founded in the late first century.

Fendoch
Fort | Orientation: 219° (South-west) | NN 9196 2830
Camp (Possible) | Orientation: Unknown | NN 9168 2878
Fortlet (Possible) | Orientation: Unknown | NN 911 278

Positioned on a natural outcrop to the south-east of the River Almond, the fort at Fendoch commands good views to the north-east and takes up the entirety of the hill on which it is located. The fort makes use of the natural topography

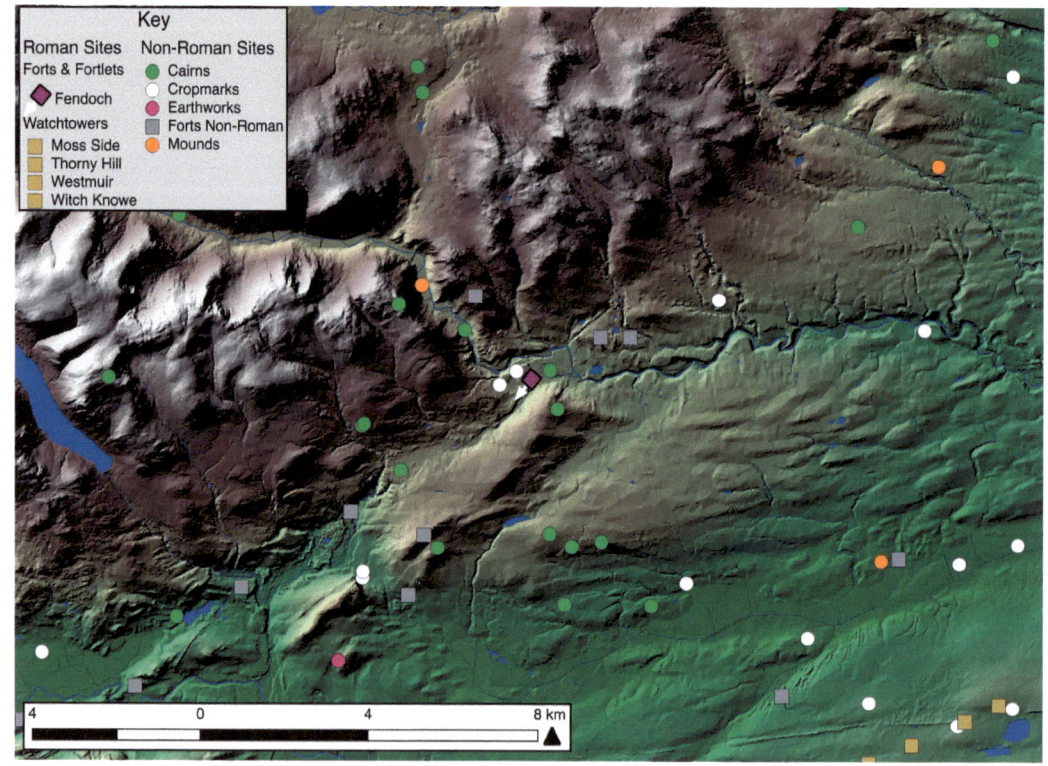

Archaeological features around Fendoch fort.

for defence. In particular, there is a steep escarpment on the south-east side of the hill. It is the most defensive site in the area, however the disadvantage is that it is overlooked to the south-west, and may have been susceptible to attack. The possible camp (often referred to as the redoubt) is to the north-east of the fort and is recorded as early as 1778, although only appears to have defences on three sides. The redoubt has not been formally investigated and it remains to be seen if it has Roman origins, or, as has been speculated, it is an indigenous site. If it is Roman, then it would seem likely that it would date to the same period as the nearby fort. Around 0.6 kilometres to the south-east of the fort is a possible fortlet site; however, it has not been excavated and it is unclear if this is Roman or not. The excavations of the 1930s established a plan of the interior of the fort, revealing the *principia* and demonstrating the fort faced south-east. The orientation was restricted by the outcrop on which it is located. Not enough of the defences of the camp have been identified to calculate the orientation. The fort excavations uncovered pottery datable to the latter half of the first century.

Glenbank

Fortlet | Orientation: 325° (North-west) | NN 8121 0570

The fortlet at Glenbank is situated on a hill, making use of the natural ridge along which the Roman road was constructed, and commands good views to the north-west, the direction that the entrance faces. The Roman road runs in front of the fortlet entrance. To the north is the Allan Water, while immediately to the east is the Glassingbeg Burn, and the Todhill Burn is to the west. No datable evidence has been recovered at this site, however it is assumed it is Flavian based on the dating of similar structures in the area.

Gourdie, Steed Stalls

Camp | Orientation: Unknown | NO 1151 4271

Located towards the summit of a steep hill, the site at Gourdie is above a quarry, which may have been used for the construction of the nearby Inchtuthil legionary fortress. There are no confirmed Roman roads nearby, but the road approaching the quarry to the south of the camp is possibly of Roman origin, although this has not been confirmed. The camp has several curiosities: it has a clear dividing line across the middle of the site; it has the trough-like features that have not been noted at other camps; and it appears to 'guard' the quarry on the lower slopes, but also has limited views to the north. The site is impractically placed to look after the quarry or to process the rock. The quarry itself is linked to the fortress but no modern spectral analysis has taken place to confirm the rocks used in the defences have come from Gourdie. The cropmarks imply the site is Roman, but the dividing line is something not seen on other Flavian sites in Scotland. This square site is level, and it is not possible to calculate which way it faces. The camp is assumed to date to the Flavian period because of its location next to a quarry and Inchtuthil legionary fortress.

Inchtuthil

Legionary Fortress | Orientation: 201° (South) | NO 1251 3971
Camp I | Orientation: Unknown | NO 1165 3934
Camp II | Orientation: Unknown | NO 1197 3945

The fortress and the camps are constructed on a raised natural platform, making use of this for defence; there has been river erosion to the northern side of the site, as part of the fortress defences have crumbled away. The peninsula is surrounded by the Tay to the south, although the river appears to have once flowed to the north, although whether or not this was contemporary with Roman occupation of the site is unclear. The fortress commands better views to the rear of the site than the direction in which it faces, while camp I may face north, taking advantage of these views. Elsewhere on the plateau are at least two camps, and at least one

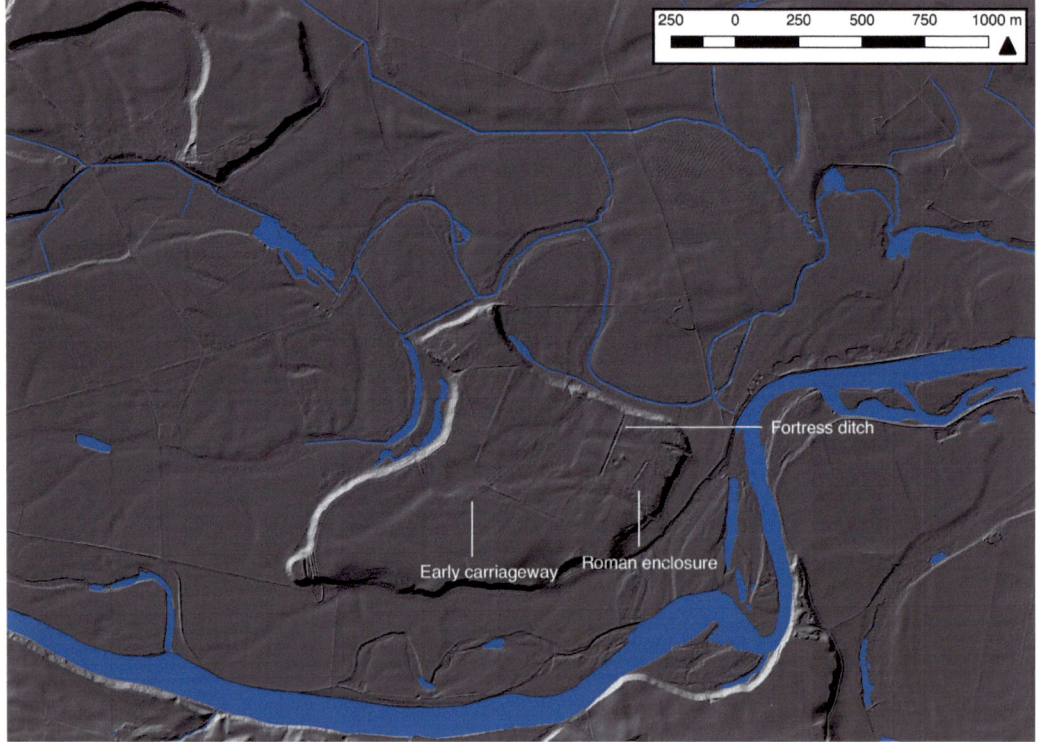

LiDAR image of Inchtuthil legionary fortress.

indigenous fort. There are no known Roman roads in the vicinity of the peninsula. The site has been excavated and geophysically surveyed, indicating that the fortress faced south, towards the River Tay as it currently flows. The excavated *principia* is smaller than the designated space, and is on a marginally different alignment to the rest of the fortress, so may be part of an earlier fort or could be an earlier structure that was intended to be expanded during construction of the overall site. The north, west and south sides of camp I are visible in aerial imagery, with a partial section of the east side identified. If this is correct, the camp faced north or south. Assuming the possible third camp is a reduction of camp II, then the former would have been playing card shaped and likely to have faced north-east or south-west. Some suggest that camp I could have been constructed by a reconnaissance force for survey as it is sited on the highest point of the peninsula. The fortress has been dated to the Flavian period from excavation finds, while the camps are also assumed to date to the first century due to their proximity to the fortress, and as they are comparable in size with other camps of this period.

Kaims Castle

Fortlet | Orientation: 121° (South-east) | NN 8608 1295

The fortlet is located on a small hillside, making use of the natural topography. Like Glenbank, Kaims Castle is a small fortlet, which commands excellent views

Kaims Castle fortlet.

of the surrounding area – almost 365°. The original excavations by Christison uncovered the layout of the single gate, which faces south-east, along the Roman road. There is a lack of datable evidence from the fortlet, but its proximity to Ardoch and its similarities to Roman sites at Old Burrow and Martinhoe in Devon suggest it is likely to be Flavian, and potentially reoccupied in the Antonine period.

Strageath
Fort | Orientation: 270° (West) | NN 8980 1800

Located on a gentle rise on a fairly flat hill at around 35 metres high, the River Earn loops around the east of the fort, which the site makes use of for defence. The site is relatively low, so may flood at certain times of the year. With possible evidence of multi-phase occupation, Strageath is west of the river and commands limited views of the area. The Roman road runs to the west of the site, on a north trajectory, but hasn't been widely traced in the area. The fort has been extensively excavated, indicating the fort was orientated west. The final plan drawn up by the excavators shows the internal structures are on a slightly different angle to the surrounding defensive works, indicating the plan is either inaccurate (showing sites of different phases interpreted as being contemporaneous). Alternatively, the fragmented excavation technique has led to a skewed plan. In 1969, the first datable find for the site was recovered and dated to the second century; however, subsequent discoveries over a fourteen-year period have yielded evidence of multi-phase occupation, including Flavian and Antonine activity, with evidence of two forts from the latter period. Datable evidence includes coins, pottery, and glass.

Renfrewshire

Barochan Hill
Fort | Orientation: 263° (West) | NS 41480 69060

At 70 metres at the highest point, there is a gentle rise of around 5 metres between the highest and lowest parts of the fort at Barochan Hill. There is little natural topography to improve defences, although to the north the hill falls away to a glen, while modern quarry disturbance is to the immediate north-east. The site is surrounded by several hill forts. With clear views to the east, the fort faces west and possibly towards the undated hill fort at Barochan Cross. There are views of the River Clyde to the north, while to the north-west and west are blocked by various hills, including Barscube Hill, but these are not so close they would pose a threat to the site. Views to the south and

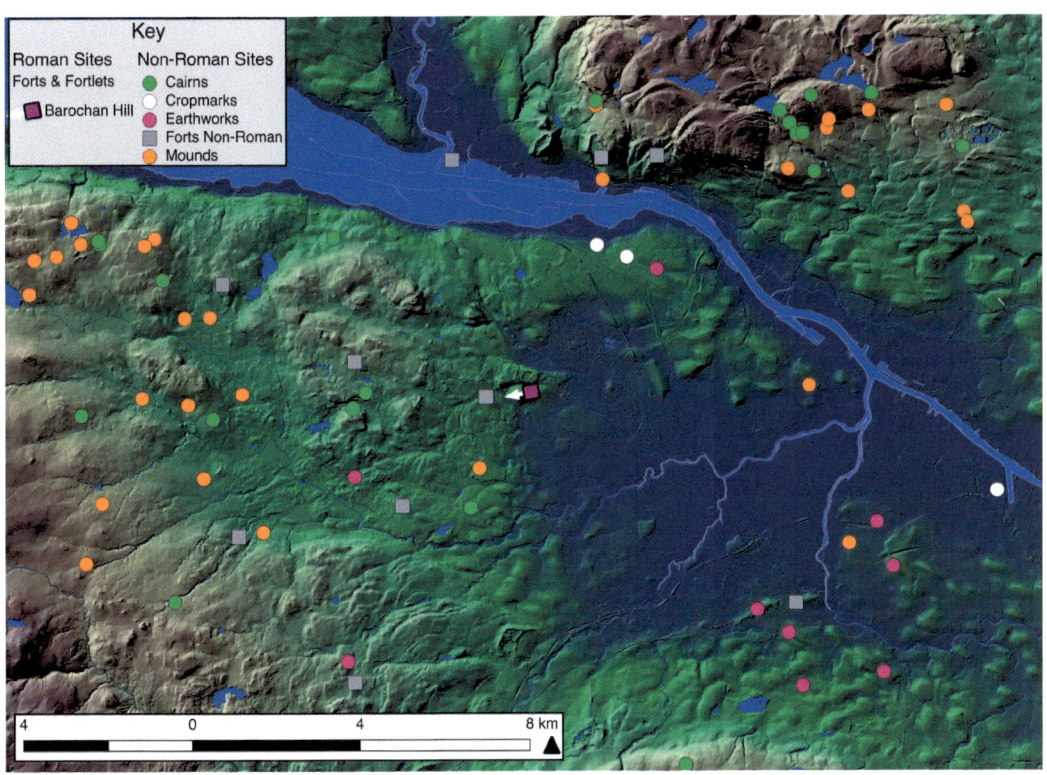

Archaeological features around Barochan Hill Roman fort.

west are considerably clearer. It seems unlikely the fort was located in this position to primarily 'guard' this section of the Clyde, which is 2.3 kilometres away. There are no known Roman roads in the immediate vicinity. Excavating the southern half of the fort, Newall uncovered the south-east corner of a major building, which led him to the conclusion that the fort faced west. The published excavation plans are not clear, but the building seems likely to have been part of the central range (the *praetorium*, *principia* and *horrea*). As there is no building plan, it is unclear whether or not it was the granary or the *praetorium* that was uncovered; the foundations of the former should be easily identifiable, but as Newall does not note this, it seems likely he may have uncovered the *praetorium*. If so, then the fort is likely to face east, not west, which would mean it faces into the annexe, which is unusual but not unheard of. It is worth noting the positioning of the *porta dextra* and *porta sinistra* two thirds of the length of the fort towards the west, which would indicate the *via praetoria* runs towards the east, indicating this is the direction which the fort faces. To date, the internal layout of the fort has not been uncovered, but from the positioning of the *porta dextra* and *porta sinistra* gates, the fort is orientated west. Pottery fragments uncovered on the site indicate a Flavian occupation date.

Scottish Borders

Cappuck
Fort | Orientation: Unknown | NT 6950 2123

The fort, or more likely fortlet, is located on a slight rise next to the Oxnam Water, where it is joined by the Cringle Burn, and was possibly constructed to protect the river crossing of the main western arterial route in Roman times. The fort is located towards the bottom of the river valley, where Dere Street runs down the hill to cross the Oxnam Water, before heading uphill on the other bank. There is post-Roman evidence that the river has moved course and eroded the fort, so any crossing points may have been in a different location or eroded. The site has limited views except on the east side. Although the *principia* has been excavated at the end of the nineteenth century and again eighteen years later, it is not possible to suggest which direction this site faces. The original excavations found no datable evidence, but subsequent work uncovered first-century pottery, with the excavator hypothesising that there were two phases of Flavian occupation.

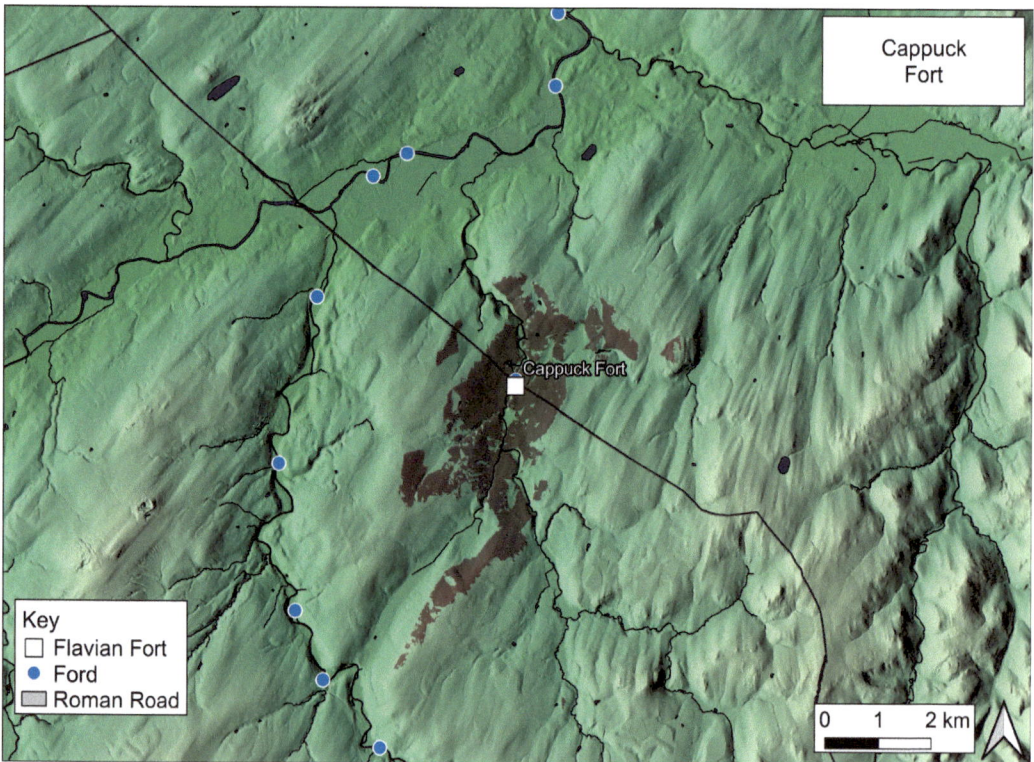

Visible area (dark shading) from Cappuck fort.

Castlecraig
Camp | Orientation: Unknown | NT 1250 4450

Built on a ridge, which is itself on the lower slopes of a hill, there are two camps at Castlecraig, with the second one inside the first, indicating two different occupation periods. Not all of the defences have been identified, however, the gate on the south-eastern side indicates that it may face north-west. If the camp is facing the former direction then it may be overlooking the Roman road, which is assumed to pass by the site to the south, although there is little evidence to confirm this route. The camp is believed to be Flavian because of its proximity to other similar sites, and because it is located next to the road.

Easter Happrew
Fort | Orientation: 140° (South-east) | NT 19469 40111

Positioned on a hillside spur with a slight slope, the fort is guarding the point where the Lyne Water meets the River Tweed. Its positioning overlooking the confluence and on a spur indicates that the fort is taking full defensive advantage of the natural topography. Easter Happrew is a square fort with a single ditch reminiscent of the

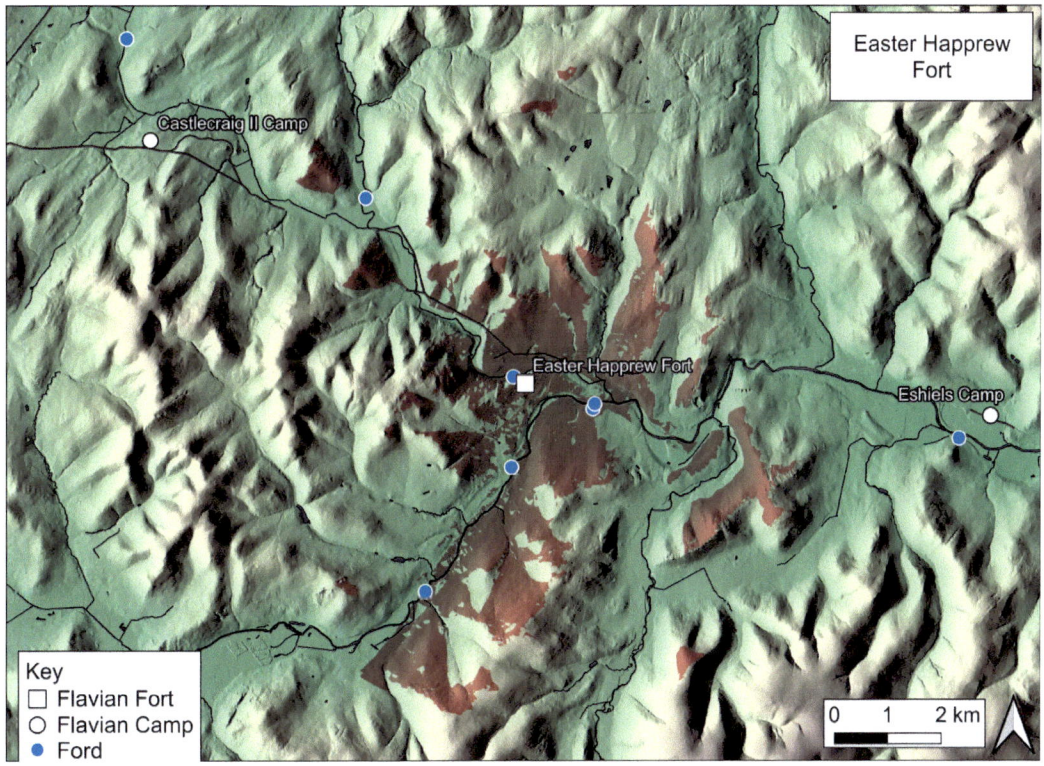

Visible area (red shading) from Easter Happrew fort.

first-century forts at Bochastle, Newstead and Birrens. It seems likely that it was positioned here to guard over the river junction and any routes east–west, although the road on the north bank of the Lyne (where there are other, later fortifications) is likely to date from the Antonine period, but there may have been an earlier route. The fort also has good views in the direction it faces, south, down the valley of the Tweed, which may suggest that there was a thoroughfare in this direction. The site is one of the only ones in Scotland of this period to yield potential evidence for a *mansio* (a sort of Roman hotel), which may be further evidence that the fort was located on or near a main route. During the 1956 excavations the *praetorium* was uncovered, and along with the positioning of the east gate, the excavator concluded that the fort faced south (or more correctly, south-east). The excavator did not publish a comprehensive plan of the internal buildings in relation to the defences, so it has not been possible to confirm their findings. Originally photographed by the RAF in mid-twentieth century, the fort was only spotted from these in 1955 and excavated the following year. The work revealed a single coin of Vespasian (AD 71), giving a Flavian occupation date for the site. The excavators suggested that the fort was abandoned in AD 90 and replaced by the fort across the river at Lyne.

Eshiels
Camps | Orientation: 204° (South-west) | NT 28150 39530

The two Eshiels camps are sited on a plain just above the Tweed, but in the shadow of mountains to the north and south, with the former possibly posing a

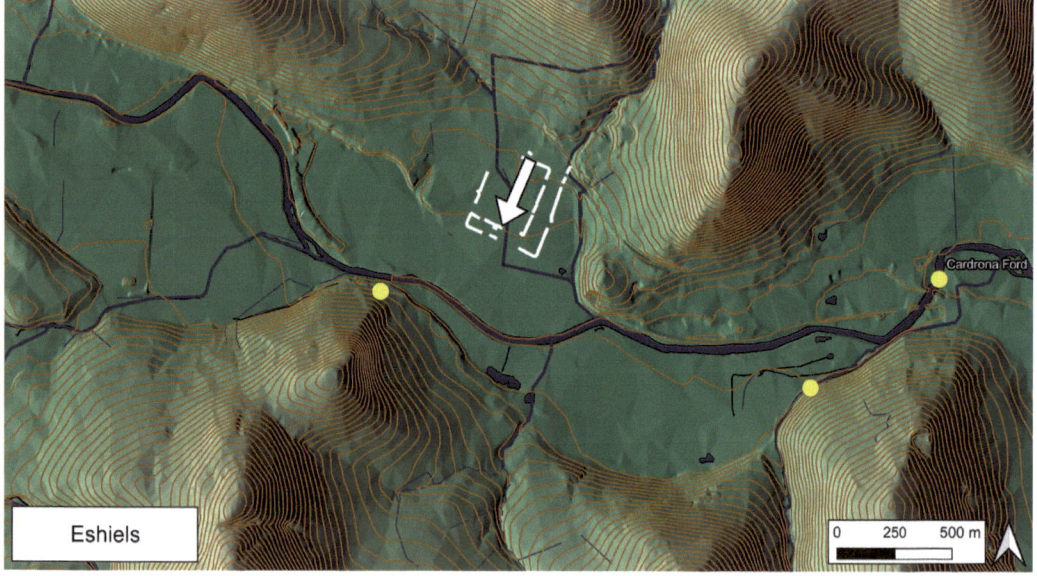

The camps at Eshiels.

security risk to the site. Although there are two camps constructed on top of each other, the long/short axis of both can be identified, however it is not possible to base orientation on the gates alone as the one on the north-eastern side may be shared. The highest point is on the north-eastern side, indicating that the site faces south-west. The site only has good views to the south and west. The camps may face a crossing point over the river, although there is no clear route for it to take on the south bank other than running parallel with the river. Aerial photographs taken in 1992 have indicated that the entrance ditch on the eastern side has a parrot-beak style gate giving a first-century foundation date for the site.

Newstead
Fort I | Orientation: Unknown | NT 56980 34410
Fort II | Orientation: 253° (West) | NT 56980 34410
Camp I (Possible) | Orientation: 24° (North-east) |): NT 57400 34100
Camp II (Possible) | Orientation: Unknown | NT 57400 34100

The sites at Newstead are all surrounded by higher ground, while the fort and camps are located on a more level site, near a crossing point over the River Tweed.

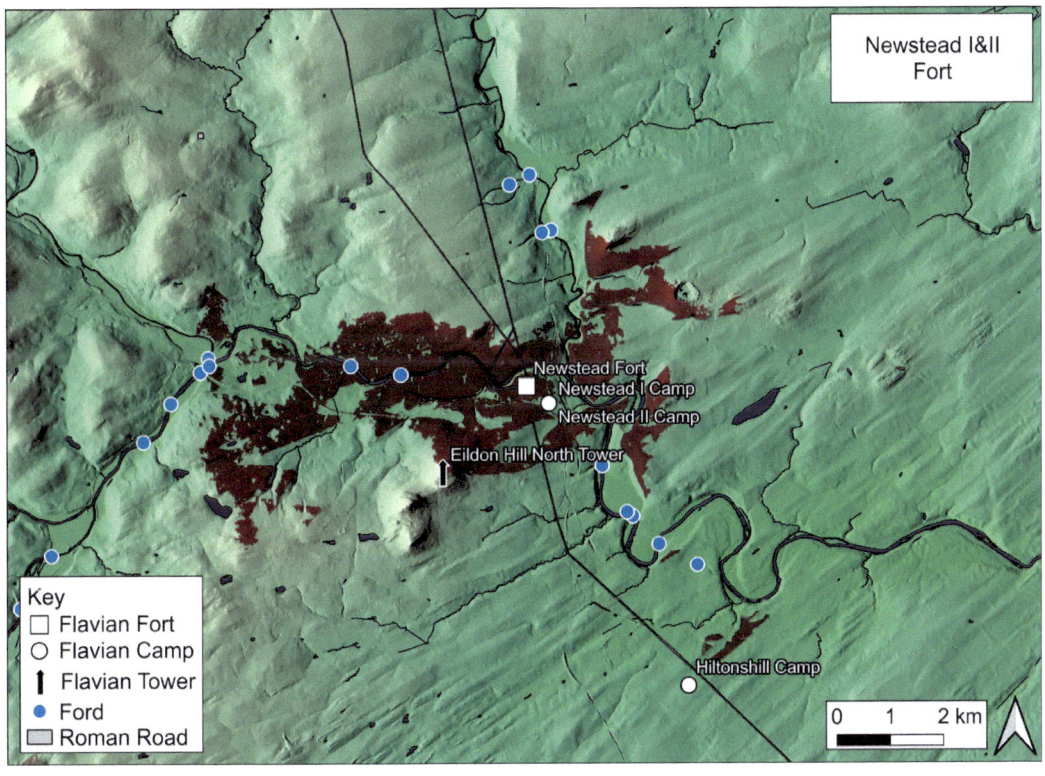

Combined visible area (dark shading) from the Newstead forts.

The Eildon Hills, to the south-west, are fairly prominent in the local landscape, and there are several fortifications here, although they would not have been able to fire into the Roman sites. On Eildon Hill North appears to be a Roman tower, implying that the hill was secured in the Roman period. Dere Street approaches the Newstead sites from the south-east and then passes through the sites and crosses the river at some unknown point. There is some speculation that the road may cross the river further to the west than the current projection – the route of the road through the surrounding area is unconfirmed. The sites are on a hill, and it seems unlikely that the river was crossed at this point via a ford because of the steepness down to the water level. It seems more likely that a bridge was constructed here, or the waterway was crossed further upstream. Fort I is an unusual shape, and the internal layout was never fully excavated and confirmed, so although the indication is that the fort faces east, there is not enough evidence to confirm this. The unusual shape is reflected in several other sites, such as at Bochastle and Milton. The earliest two phases of the fort were constructed on top of each other, with excavation revealing the internal layout of the later fort II, although this has been questioned by some archaeologists. It indicates that the fort faced east. The gates on the long axis of camp I are known, indicating it faces north-east, while only two sides of the defences of camp II are not known, so it is not possible to say which direction it faces. The sites were initially excavated in the early part of the twentieth century, with follow up excavations in the 1940s, and modern reinterpretation of the site in 2015. The original excavations led to the discovery of the multi-phase occupation of the site, as well as Flavian activity, as evidenced by the extensive pottery finds. The relationships and dating between the various camps at Newstead is complicated due to the sites overlying each other, and a lack of finds. However, the camps are assumed to be Flavian because they are beneath the other sites, and assumed to be contemporary with the early forts.

Oakwood
Fort | Orientation: 70° (East) | NT 4250 2491
Camp | Orientation: 210° (South-west) | NT 4248 2544

Overlooking the river valley to the west, the fort and camp are both also overlooked by hills to the south, although these are not high enough to pose a threat to either site. Reminiscent of the fort at Bochastle, and to an extent Milton and Newstead, the layout of Oakwood fort is square rather than the traditional playing card shape. However, unlike the former, excavators could define the internal roads, giving an orientation for the site. The road approaches the fort from the south, but beyond this to the north, its route is unknown. Unusually, the fort is not facing the river or potential crossing point. Both the fort and the camp are located in the hills, implying that it was guarding the area rather than a particular route, as this seems more likely to be lower down the hill in the river valley. During the excavations of the fort, the excavators also recorded the camp, noting the gates were towards the lower half of the southern end, indicating it faces south-west. During excavation of the fort site, several pottery fragments were recovered from a trench excavated behind the rampart, which they dated to the Flavian period. Although no datable evidence has been found for the camp, the excavators have speculated that it was used as a labour site during the construction of the fort, implying construction in the Flavian period.

Stirling

Bochastle
Fort | Orientation: Unknown | NN 6142 0790
Camp | Orientation: Unknown | NN 6117 0772

The sites at Bochastle are located to the south of the Endrick Water, and are between 70 and 80 metres above sea level, on a flat plane, and making limited use of the natural topography with the river at the northern end of the site. It is highly likely the area may have been prone to flooding during wet periods; the adjacent Gobhain Burn is recorded on the 1860 Ordnance Survey map as being liable to flood. The site is surrounded by hills, with the fortifications located in the river valley instead of on one of the nearby hills, which would have afforded it a more defensive position. Views are restricted, with primary vision limited to the river valleys to the east, south-west, and north-west. No roads have been identified near Bochastle. Geophysical survey has highlighted preserved internal buildings, which indicate the fort is likely, but not confirmed, as orientated north. Given both camps are playing card shaped, they are likely to have either faced north or south.

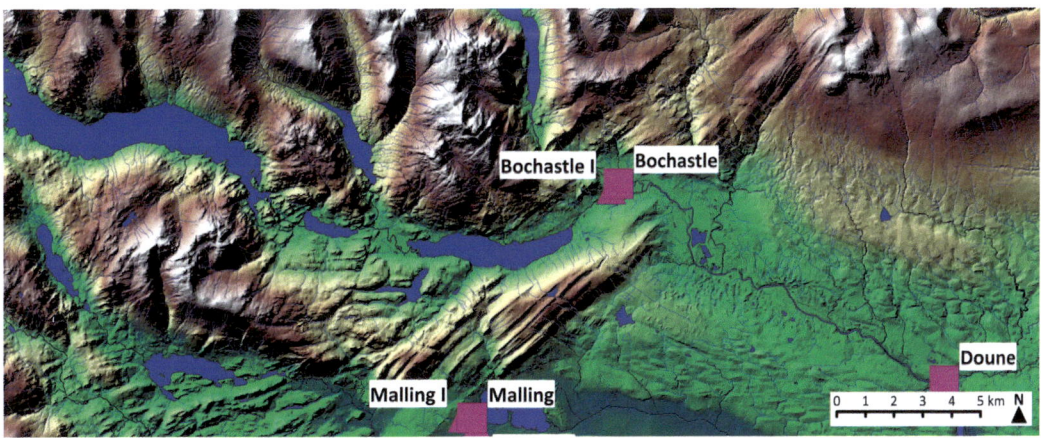

Roman sites in Stirlingshire.

Excavation in the 1940s and 1950s led to speculation that there were two phases of fort construction during the Flavian period. Subsequent work found evidence the camp and fort intersect at the north-east corner, indicating it unlikely that the two were not in use at the same time. Little datable evidence was revealed until the end of excavations, with coarse first-century pottery. Geophysical survey of the camps has revealed first-century, parrot-beak gates.

Doune

Fort | Orientation: 124° (South-east) | NN 7273 0130

Located on a hillside overlooking where the Ardoch Burn meets the River Teith, Doune has limited views to the south-west, the direction in which it faces. The fort is located on a hill and is surrounded by water on three sides, and makes full use of the defensive topography provided by the river valleys. It is not immediately overlooked by higher ground. Woolliscroft and Hoffmann discuss the orientation of Doune in relation to an unpublished excavation (which was not undertaken by the authors) where preliminary findings noted the discovery of buildings, which would normally be located in the central range. The buildings therefore face onto the *via principalis*, even though this

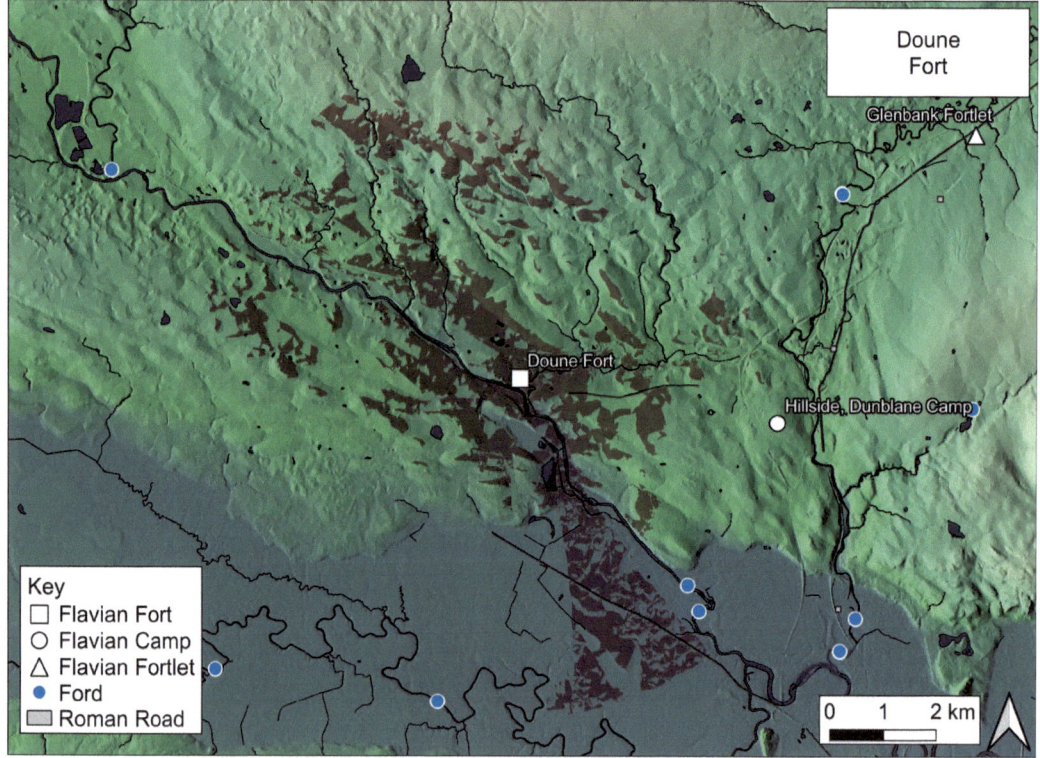

Visible area (dark shading) from Doune fort.

would be along the long axis of the site, which would be unusual but indicates the fort faced north-east. This is similar to Dalginross I, however excavations in the centre of the fort have indicated the *via principalis* would be blocked by buildings, so it is more likely the fort follows the usual internal pattern and would actually face south-east. Work in 2010 has identified the south-west and north-west gates of the fort, with the south-west gate a third of the way along the long axis, indicating the *praetentura* is in the eastern section of the site, and so the fort faces south-east. The fort has a triple ditch system on the east side, with the terminals curving inwards, parrot-beak style, while excavations in 1999 uncovered first-century pottery.

Drumquhassle
Fort | Orientation: 154° (South-east) | NS 48430 87444

Commanding good views of the surrounding area, particularly towards Loch Lomond (5 kilometres north-west), the fort itself is facing south-east, almost (but not quite) down the Altquhur Burn valley. The site is around 59 metres high and is on a hillside, dropping around 10 metres at its lowest point. Immediately to the north the hill peaks at 70 metres, though modern quarrying has disrupted this

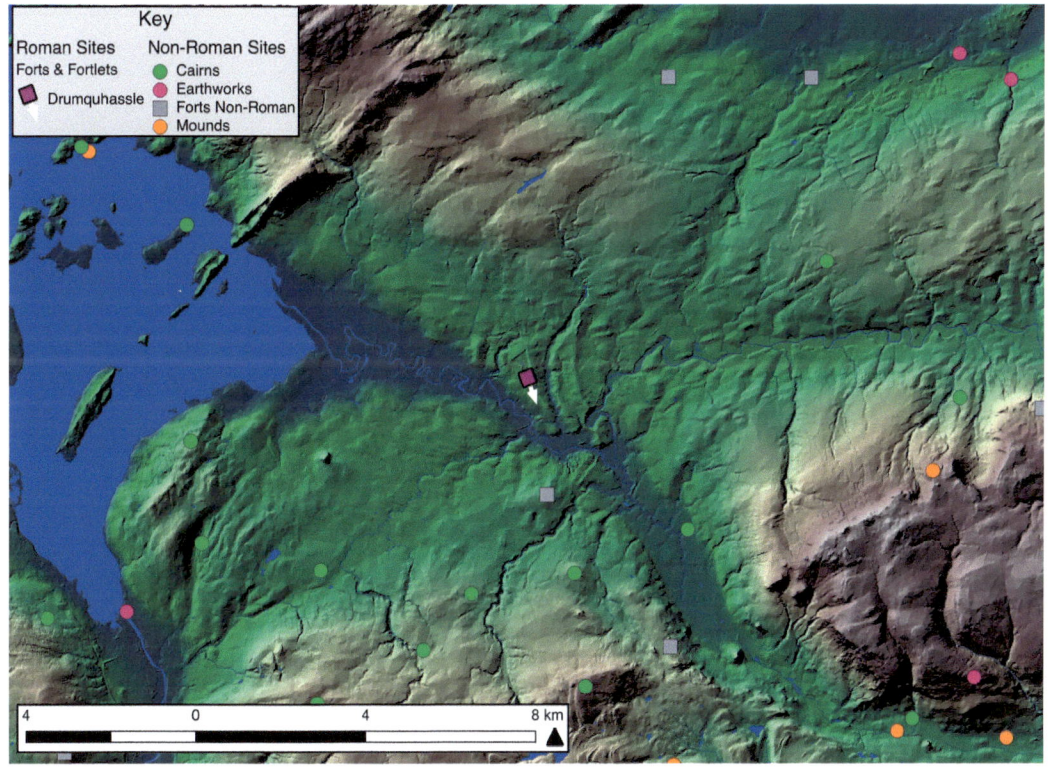

Archaeological features around Drumquhassle fort.

79

area, but it would appear the hillside originally fell away gradually in this direction. Located on the highest point, the immediate area around the site is hilly and makes use of the natural topography. Geophysical survey has indicated the west gate of the fort was located two thirds of the way along the long axis and so the fort faces south-east. It is almost facing the indigenous hill fort of Quinloch Muir (NS 5150 8134), covering 0.07 hectares and around 4 kilometres south-east. Although undated, it was noted in 1957 that it had the 'characteristic of a small stone-walled fort', with additional outer defence works (earth and stone banks, along with rock cut ditches), which were to the north-west of the site (and potentially facing Drumquhassle). If the fort was orientated a little more to the south-east, it would face down the valley of the Altquhur Burn. As the site at Quinloch Muir is so small, it seems unlikely that it would have contained a large enough populace to pose a threat to the Roman fort, although it appears to have had strong defences on the side facing it. It is unclear if the fort would have been contemporary with occupation at Drumquhassle. Excavation of the ramparts uncovered late first-century pottery in 1978, while field walking finds uncovered between 1998 and 2000 have included coins from that period. Furthermore, geophysical survey has revealed parrot-beak gates, supporting a Flavian date.

Hillside, Dunblane
Camp I | Orientation: 156° (North-east) | NN 775 005
Camp II | Orientation: Unknown | NN 775 005

Located on the side of a hill at 114 metres high, the sites appear to make some use of the natural topography for defence, particularly as the surrounding hills appear to have been too steep for the construction of camps. The camps may have been overlooked, particularly to the east, but separated by the valley of the Allan Water. The camps, which are constructed one inside the other, are located nearby to the Roman fort at Doune, while Ardoch is just under a day's march away. The area around the camps has been heavily developed in the past twenty years, and is now covered by modern housing. There are no confirmed Roman roads nearby. Camp I is playing card shaped with the north-east and south-west sides forming the long axis, which also has some gaps (possible entrances). This, along with the highest point being on the north, indicates that camp I faces south-east. With the western defences unidentified, along with a lack of gates (other than on the north side), it is not possible to calculate the orientation of camp II. The only indigenous site nearby is the small indigenous hill fort at Gallow Hill (NS 7825 9845). Oval in shape, this indigenous fort has an interior of 0.15 hectares, surrounded by a single rampart. A first-century Roman quern stone was found on the top course of the fort wall in the 1950s, which, it has been speculated, was reused by the occupants

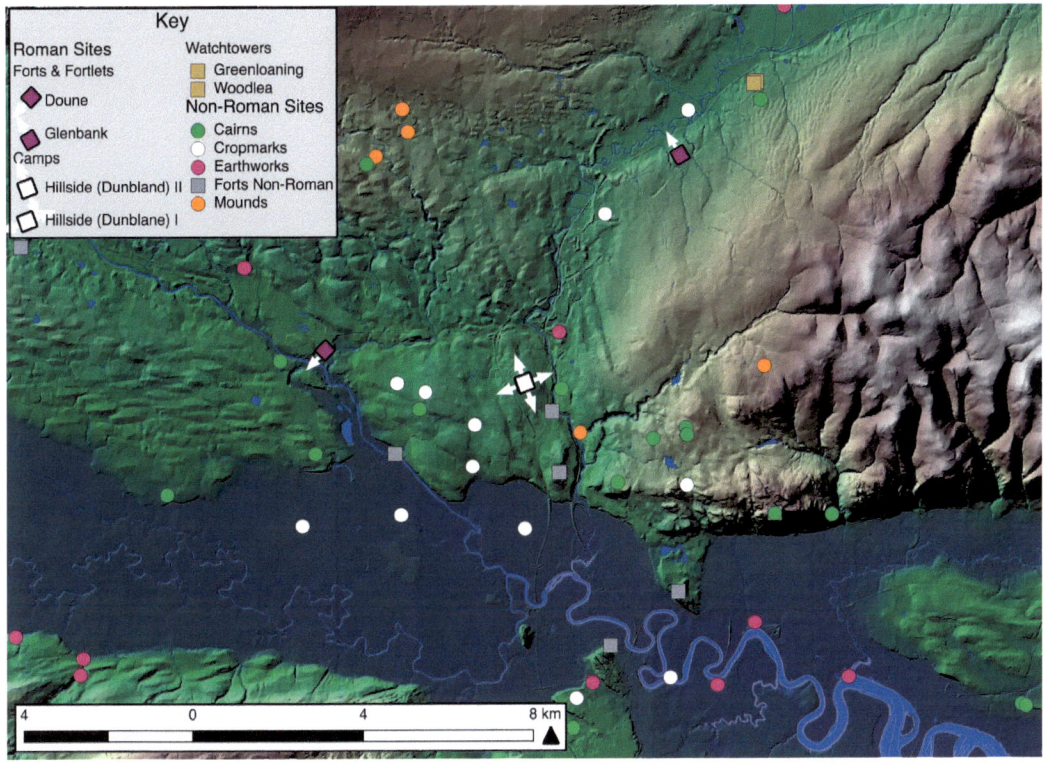

Archaeological features around the camps at Dunblane.

in the site after the Roman period as it had been modified, something that was comparable with similar objects found on other sites dating to the post-Roman period. As the quern stone was found on the top course of the walls, it is not possible to say how it got to the site, and cannot be used as evidence of occupation at the same time as the Roman camps. Camp I (the larger site) has gates protected by *tituli*, which suggests it is Flavian in date. Camp II, within the boundaries of the first camp, also shares the western defences and may be Flavian, given that *titulus* guarding the eastern and western gates.

Malling
Fort | Orientation: 67° (North-east) | NN 56400 00060
Camp I | Orientation: Unknown | NS 56560 99810
Camp II | Orientation: Unknown | NN 56070 00080

The sites at Malling are situated on the western shore of the Lake of Menteith, around 20 metres above sea level, and on a gentle rise. They are located in an area not naturally defensive, but they make use of the shore of the lake, assuming it was of a similar expanse in the Roman period. The eastern defences of the fort are untraced and may either lie under the waters of the lake, or may not have existed (the waters being used as a defensive measure). The Menteith Hills run to the north of the site, indicating the fort and camps would have been overlooked, but out of reach of any attacks from these positions. The sites have limited visibility. Some of the internal structures of the fort have been identified through aerial photography, indicating that it faced north-east. Camp I is rhomboid, with the north-west gate being centred on the short axis and another identified in the opposite south-east side; this gate is a third of the way along the bank (towards the north-east) and the camp faces north-west or south-east. Malling II is squarer, with only a single north-east gate clearly identified, although there are potential gaps in the other sides of the defences. The fort (and possibly Malling II) face towards Tamnafalloch hill fort (NN 6291 0084). Prior to 1898, a sword and chainmail were found near the indigenous site, but the context is unknown and the objects undated. Located on a hillock, the plan of the indigenous site is oval, surrounded by a single ditch and rampart, and encompassing an area of 0.24 hectares. There is an entrance to the east, facing towards an unexplored set of earthworks. The rampart was excavated in the twenty-first century, with charcoal recovered dating to the Late Bronze Age. Although no artefacts have

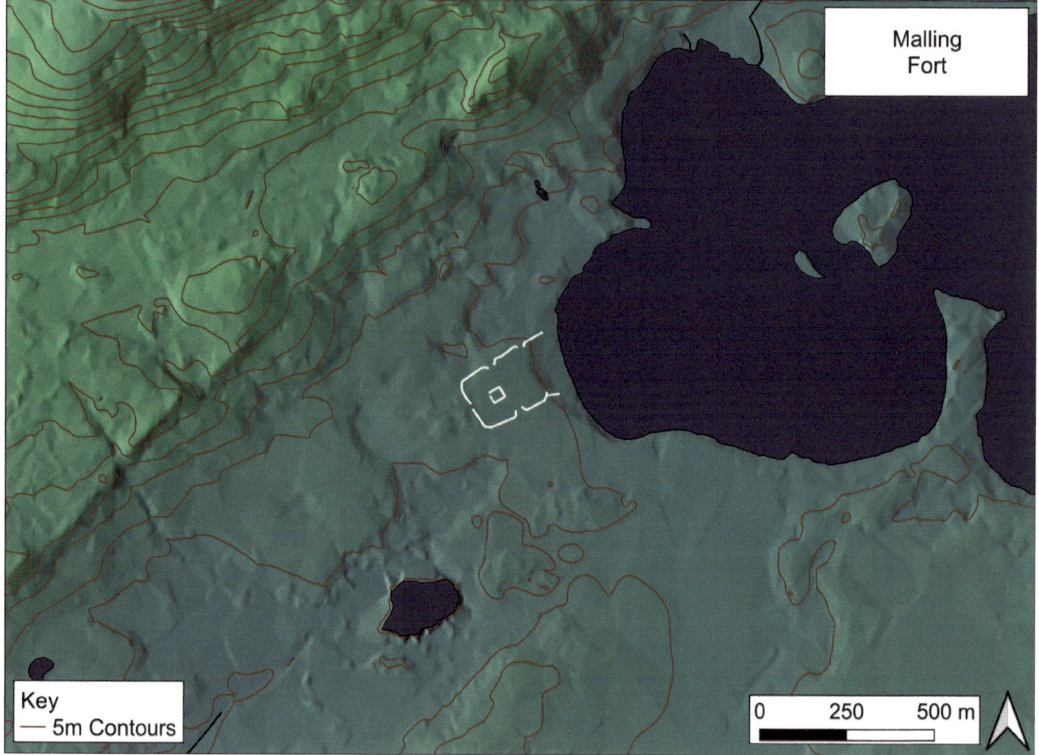

The fort at Malling on the Lake of Menteith.

been uncovered to date the Roman fort, it is believed to be Flavian due to its proximity to the camps. Camp I is presumed to be Flavian due to its parrot-beak gates. It has been speculated that camp II may have also have had this type of entrances due to an indication of a bank at an angle on the north-west gate of the site.

West Lothian

Castle Greg
Fortlet | Orientation: 66° (North-east) | NT 05020 59250

Castle Greg fortlet is on a level piece of land, overlooked by hills to the east, although there would have been no danger of attack from these. The Crosswood Burn runs to the east of the site and there are several tributaries. There is some debate if there is a road near the fortlet. Some archaeologists have argued that there is no road and that the site was built and abandoned (in the Flavian period) before there was a road constructed. Geophysical evidence has indicated that the

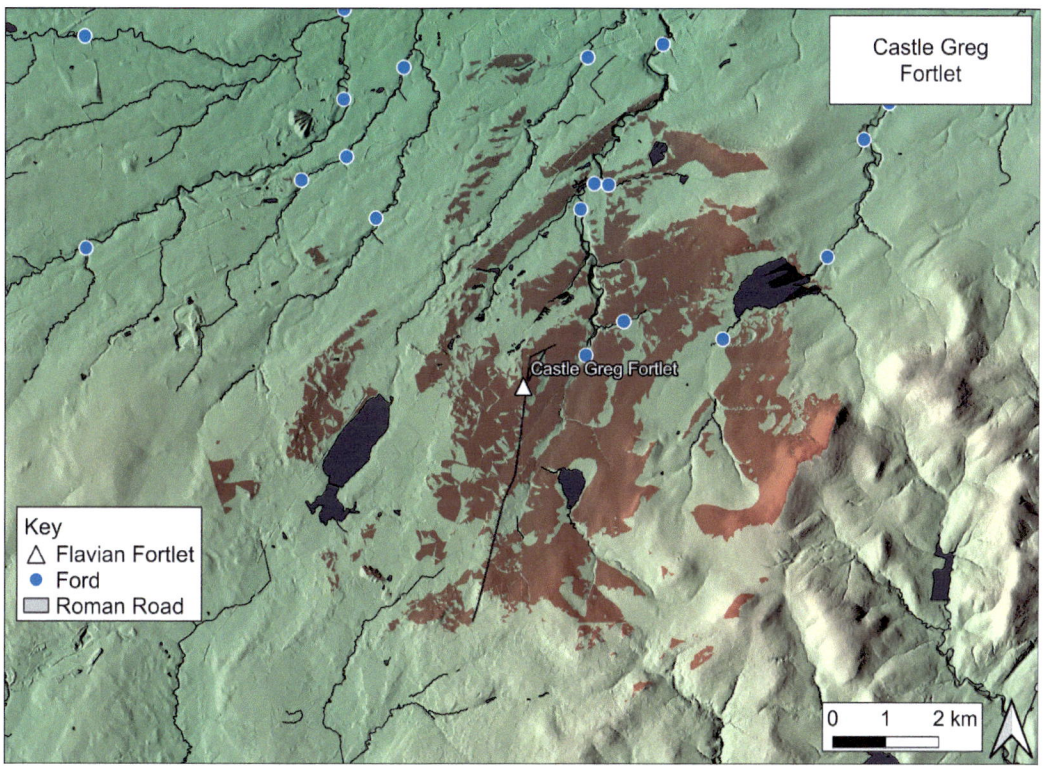

Visible area (dark shading) from Castle Greg fortlet.

track or road inside the fortlet leaves the site and heads, according to one person, towards a road, a small section of which may have been dug up in the nineteenth century and revealed to be Roman – this is what the site is orientated towards. Both theories are possible, and it seems likely that only further research will confirm which is correct. The fortlet entrance is facing north-east. The well-preserved fortlet was recorded in the *Old Statistical Account,* and first explored in the middle of the nineteenth century revealing pottery and coins, the latter having a range of dates including Vespasian, Hadrian, and Antoninus Pius. The fortlet also has a parrot-beak-style gate, indicating a first-century date.

Bibliography

There are many books which detail the archaeology and history of Roman Scotland. The texts listed here are some of the most relevant volumes covering first-century activity in northern Britain. See also the volumes listed under the Individual Site Sources.

Abercromby, J., 'Account of the Excavation of the Roman Station at Inchtuthil, Perthshire Undertaken by the Society of Antiquaries in Scotland in 1901', *Proceedings of the Society of Antiquaries of Scotland*, 36 (1902) pp. 182–203.

Birley, A. (trans), *Tacitus: Agricola and Germany* (Oxford: Oxford University Press, 2009).

Bishop, M. C., *Handbook to Roman Legionary Fortresses* (Barnsley: Pen & Sword Military, 2013).

Bishop, M. C., *The Secret History of the Roman Roads of Britain* (Barnsley: Pen & Sword Books, 2014).

Breeze, D., 'Agricola in the Highlands?' *PSAS*, 120 (1990), pp. 55–60.

Breeze, D. J., *Edge of Empire: Scotland's Roman Frontier* (Birlinn, Edinburgh, 2008).

Breeze, D. J., *The Northern Frontiers of Roman Britain* (Batsford Academic & Educational, London, 1993).

Breeze, D. J., 'Why did the Romans fail to conquer Scotland?' *Proceedings of the Society of Antiquaries of Scotland*, 118 (1988), pp. 3–22.

Crawford, O. G. S., *Topography of Roman Scotland North of the Antonine Wall* (Cambridge: Cambridge University Press, 1949).

Davies, H., *Roads in Roman Britain* (Stroud: Tempus, 2002).

Dilke, O. A. W., *The Roman Land Surveyors: An Introduction to the Agrimensores* (Newton Abbot: David & Charles, 1971).

Frere, S. S. & St Joseph, J. K.,. *Roman Britain from the Air* (Cambridge University Press, 1983).

Graafstal, E., 'Wing-Walls and Waterworks. On the Planning and Purpose of the Antonine Wall', in D. J. Breeze & W. S. Hanson (eds.), *The Antonine Wall: Papers in Honour of Professor Lawrence Keppie* (Oxford: Archaeopress, 2020).

Hannon, N., Wilson, L. & Rohl, D. J., 'Planning the Antonine Wall: an Archaeometric Reassessment of Installation Spacing', in D. J. Breeze & W. S. Hanson (eds.), *The Antonine Wall: Papers in Honour of Professor Lawrence Keppie* (Oxford: Archaeopress, 2020), pp. 67–85.

Hanson, W. S., *Agricola and the Conquest of the North* (London: BT Batsford, 1991).

Hanson, W. S., *A Roman Frontier Fort in Scotland: Elginhaugh* (Stroud: Tempus, 2007).

Hoffmann, B., *The Roman Invasion of Britain: Archaeology Versus History* (Barnsley: Pen & Sword Archaeology, 2013).

Jones, R. H., *Roman Camps in Scotland* (Society of Antiquaries of Scotland: Edinburgh, 2011).

Keppie, L., *Scotland's Roman Remains* (Edinburgh: John Donald Publishers, 1998).

Maxwell, G. S., 'Agricola's Campaigns: The Evidence of the Temporary Camps', in J. Kenworthy (ed.) *Agricola's Campaigns in Scotland* (Edinburgh: Edinburgh University Press, 1980).

Maxwell, G. S., *The Romans in Scotland* (James Thin the Mercat Press: Edinburgh, 1989).

Maxwell, G. S., *A Battle Lost: Romans and Caledonians at Mons Graupius* (Edinburgh University Press: Edinburgh, 1990).

Mercer, R., *Native and Roman on the Northern Frontier: Excavations and Survey in a Later Prehistoric Landscape in Upper Eskdale, Dumfriesshire* (Edinburgh: Society of Antiquaries of Scotland, 2018).

Miller, S. N. (ed.), *The Roman Occupation of South Western Scotland* (Glasgow University Publications: Glasgow, 1952).

Milner, N. P. (ed.), *Vegetius: Epitome of Military Science (Epitoma De Re Militari)* 3rd ed. (Liverpool: Liverpool University Press, 2001).

Symonds, M., *Protecting the Empire: Fortlets, Frontiers and the Quest for Post-Conquest Security* (Cambridge: Cambridge University Press, 2018).

The Chevalier de Johnstone, *A Memoir of the Forty-Five* (London: Folio Society, 1958).

Tibbs, A., *Facing the Enemy? A GIS-Based Examination of first century Roman Fortifications in a Scottish Landscape Setting* (British Archaeological Reports: Oxford, 2022).

Tibbs, A., *Beyond the Empire: A Guide to Scotland's Roman Remains* (Robert Hale: Marlborough, 2019).

Woolliscroft, D. & Hoffmann, B., *Rome's First Frontier: The Flavian Occupation of Northern Scotland* (Stroud: Tempus, 2006).

Additional and Roman Sources

Archaeological Data Service (ADS), archaeologydataservice.ac.uk.

Canmore: The national record of the historic environment in Scotland, www.Canmore.org.

Chalmers, G., *Caledonia: Or a Historical and Topographical Account of North Britain* (Alexander Gardner: Paisley, 1887).

Gordon, A., *Itinerarium Septentrionale: or, a Journey Thro' Most of the Counties of Scotland, and Those in the North of England* (Alexander Gordon: 1726).

Hyginus ('Pseudo'), *De Munitionibus Castrorum* (The Fortification of the Camp).

Macdonald, G., *The Roman Wall in Scotland* (The Clarendon Press: 1934), pp. 321–322, 340, 478.

Maitland, W., *History and Antiquities of Scotland* (A. Millar: London, 1757).

Roy, W., *Military Antiquities of the Romans in North Britain* (W. Bulmer & Co.: London, 1793).

Tacitus, Agricola.

Tacitus, *Annals.*

Tacitus, *Historiae* (Histories).

The Roman Gask Project, www.theromangaskproject.org.

The Statistical Account of Scotland, Drawn Up from the Communications of the Ministers of the Different Parishes (known as *The Old Statistical Account of Scotland*), (Edinburgh: 1791–99).

Vegetius, *Epitoma De Re Militari* (Epitome of Military Science).

Individual Site Sources

The following abbreviations are used for the sources consulted for the individual site entries. Full details of the publications can be found in the Further Reading section. See also individual site entries on Canmore, in *Rome's First Frontier* (2006), *Roman Camps in Scotland* (2011), and in *Beyond the Empire* (2019).

AC	*Agricola's Campaigns: The Evidence of the Temporary Camps* (by Maxwell)
AJ	*Archaeological Journal*
AS	*Archaeologia Scotica*
BRIT	*Britannia*
DES	*Discovery & Excavation in Scotland*
GAJ	*Glasgow Archaeological Journal*
JRS	*Journal of the Society for the Promotion of Roman Studies*
OSA	*The Statistical Account of Scotland*

PSAS	*Proceedings of the Society of Antiquaries of Scotland*
RBFA	*Roman Britain from the Air* (by Frere & St Joseph)
RCS	*Roman Camps in Scotland* (by Jones)
RIS	*The Romans in Scotland* (by Maxwell)
RFF	*Rome's First Frontier: The Flavian Occupation of Northern Scotland* (by Woolliscroft & Hoffmann)
SAJ	*Scottish Archaeological Journal*
TRS	*Topography of Roman Scotland North of the Antonine Wall* (by Crawford)
ROSS	*The Roman Occupation of South Western Scotland* (ed. By Miller)
TDGNHAS	*Transactions of the Dumfriesshire and Galloway Natural History and Antiquarian Society*

Aberdeenshire

Burnfield: BRIT 15 (1984) 273 | JRS 18 (1987) 34.

Glenmailen (Ythan Wells): BRIT 1 (1970), 163–178 | JRS 59 (1969) 112–114.

Kintore: DES (1996) 8–9; (1997) 10–11; (2000) 26–33; (2001) 11; (2002) 10 JRS 59 (1969) 59 | PSAS 7 (1868) 387–394; 116 (1987) 205–209; 130 (2000) 26–33.

Cook, M., Dunbar, L., *Rituals, Roundhouses and Romans. Excavations at Kintore, Aberdeenshire 2000–2006*, Volume 1: Forest Road (Scottish Trust for Archaeological Research: Loanhead, 2008).

Cook, M., Dunbar, L., Heawood, R., *Rituals, Roundhouses and Romans. Excavations at Kintore, Aberdeenshire 2000–2006*, Volume 2: Other Sites (Scottish Trust for Archaeological Research: Loanhead, 2009).

Logie Durno: BRIT 9 (1978) 271–287 | JRS 67 (1977) 141–142 | RBFA 30–31.

Milltimber: BRIT 49 (2018) 339.

Dingwall, K., Shepherd, J., *Highway Through History: an Archaeological Journey on the Aberdeen Western Peripheral Route* (Headland Archaeology (UK) Ltd: Edinburgh, 2018).

Normandykes: BRIT 38 (2007) 254 | JRS 48 (1958) 93; 59 (1969) 118 | RCS 286.

Raedykes: AS 1 (1792) 565–569; 2 (1822) 300 | JRS 48 (1958) 51 (1961) 119–135 | PSAS 50 (1916) 317–359; 73 (1938) 250–252 | TRS 108–111.

Angus

Cardean: BRIT 7 (1976) 299; 33 (2002) 285 | DES (1966) 1; (1974) 7; (2001) 14–15; | JRS 45 (1955) 87; 63 (1973) 63 | RFF 158–164 | TRS 87–89.

Knox, J., *The Topography of the Basin of the Tay* (Edinburgh: Andrew Shortreed, 1831).

Dun: DES (1990) 40; (1974) 8 | JRS 63 (1973) 214–246 | PSAS 123 (1993) 286–290.
Inverquharity: BRIT 15 (1984) 274; 16 (1985) 263; 18 (1987) 15–16, 29 | DES (1983) 32–33; (1984) 35; (2002) 13 | RFF 165–167.
Stracathro: BRIT 1 (1970) 171–175, 273 | DES (1955) 5; (1969) 2 | JRS 45 (1955) 87; 48 (1958) 92. Woolliscroft, D. & Hoffmann, B., *Geophysical Survey of Stracathro Roman Fort* (See canmore.org, 2012).

Ayrshire

Ayr: BRIT 50 (2019) 330–349.
Girvan Mains: BRIT 9 (1978) 397–401; 13 (1982) 339; 15 (1984) 274; 9 (1978) 397–401 | DES (1993) 86; (1996) 97; (2009) 171.
Loudoun Hill: BRIT 3 (1972) 11 | DES (1947) 5; (1954) 7–8 | JRS 29 (1939) 201; 33 (1943) 71; 37 (1946) 165–182; 38 (1947) 165-166; 39 (1949) 96–115; 45 (1955) 82–91 | NSA 5 (1793) 181 | ROSS 188–191.

Dumfries and Galloway

Beattock (Bankend and Barnhill): BRIT 7 (1976) 33–38; 16 (1985) 267 | DES (1977) 53; (1984) 6 | GAJ 4 (1976) 6 | JRS 67 (1977) 133; 9 (1978) 418–419 | ROSS 113–114.
Birrens: BRIT 1 (1970) 42, 274; 3 (1972) 10; 16 (1985) 326; 28 (1997) 410–411 | DES (1964) 25; (1965) 16–17; (1966) 21; (1967) 21; (1969) 18; (1977) 41; (1996) 31; (1999) 24; (2014) 63 | JRS 41 (1951) 57–58 | PSAS 30 (1895–96) 81–199; 72 (1938) 275-347 | TDGNHAS 11 (1894–95) 55–67; 41 (1962–63) 135–155.
Robertson, A. S., *Birrens (Blatobulgium)* (T. & A. Constable: Glasgow, 1975).
Broomholm: BRIT 3 (1972) 10 | DES (1950) 8; (1956) 13–14; (1960) 26; (2016) 49–50 | TDGNHAS 25 (1947) 132–150; 28 (1951) 188–189.
Dalswinton: BRIT 3 (1972) 11; 49 (2018); 50 (2019) 285–320 | DES (2009) 59 JRS 41 (1951) 58–59, Plate VI; 45 (1955) 85–85; 48 (1958) 89; 51 (1961) 122; 55 (1965) 79; 63 (1973) 217; 67 (1977) 131–133 | ROSS 49 | TDGNHAS 34 (1954) 9–21.
Denholm (Eastcote): AC 40–41 | JRS 51 (1961) 122; 55 (1965) 78.
Drumlanrig (including Islafoot): BRIT 16 (1985) 267, 18 (1987) 19–20, 36 (2005) 401–02 | DES (2004) 35 | RIS 74.
Wessex Archaeology, *Drumlanrig Castle | Excavation (Archaeology) | Fortification*, Wessex Archaeology (2005).
Durisdeer: AC 40 | JRS 41 (1951) 40.
Fourmerkland: AC 40 | JRS 41 (1951) 60.

Gatehouse of Fleet: BRIT 3 (1972) 11 | DES (1960) 29; (1961) 35 | JRS 41 (1951) 57; 51 (1961) 161.
Glenlochar: AC 40 | BRIT 3 (1972) 11 | DES (1955) 18 | TDGNHAS 30 (1953) 1–16 Stell, G., *Dumfries and Galloway, Exploring Scotland's Heritage* (Edinburgh: RCAHMS, 1996).
Glenluce: *BRIT* 24 (1993) 281.
Kirkland: BRIT 20 (1990) 321; 24 (1993) 281.
Milton: ROSS 104–110 | TDGNHAS 24 (1947) 100–110; 25 (1948) 10–26; 26 (1949) 133–149; 27 (1950) 197–201; 28 (1950) 199–221.
Raeburnfoot: BRIT 27 (1996) 357; 40 (2009) 123–136 | DES (1947) 3; (1959) 22; (1960) 25 | TDGNHAS 14 (1898) 17–27; 24 (1947) 150–159; 39 (1962) 24–49.
Ward Law: RCS 118 | RIS 80 | ROSS 117–120.

Edinburgh

Gogar Green: BRIT 13 (1982) 94, 340; 16 (1985) 365; 18 (1987) 38–39 | DES (1984) 16.

Falkirk

Camelon: BRIT 3 (1972) 5; 10 (1979) 275; 11 (1980) 340–343 | DES (1972) 53; (1973) 52; (1975) 52; (1976) 61; (1977) 34–35; (1998) 37 | PSAS 35 (1900–01) 329–350, 350–379; 109 (1977–78) 151–165; 124 (1994) 307.
Hanson, W. S. & Maxwell, G. S.,. *Rome's North-West Frontier: The Antonine Wall* (Edinburgh: Edinburgh University Press, 1986), p. 191.
Lochlands: DES (1982) 5 | GAJ 4 (1976) 1–28 | RCS 257–261.

Lanarkshire

Carnwath: BRIT 16 (1985) 265; 18 (1987) 19 | RCS 55, 89, 138–139.
Castledykes: BRIT 15 (1984) 57–60; 19 (1988) 429–430; 20 (1989) 312 | DES (1984) 26; (1985) 40; (1986) 30; (1991) 69 | JRS 41 (1951) 57 | PSAS 52 (1918) 219 | RCS 168–169 | ROSS 127–171 | SAF (1975) 18–24.
Robertson, A. S., *The Roman Fort at Castledykes* (Oliver & Boyd, 1964).
Cold Chapel: BRIT 18 (1987) 34 | ROSS 33–34.
Cornhill: BRIT 18 (1987) 34 | GAJ 4 (1976) 6–7 | RCS 175.
Crawford: BRIT 3 (1972) 10; 18 (1987) 40; 27 (1996) 357 | GAJ 4 (1976) 28 | PSAS 103 (1970–71) 115 | ROS 113–114.

Kirkhouse: BRIT 15 (1984) 276; 17 (1986) 371, 374.

Lamington: AC 40–41 | ROSS 35.

Mollins: BRIT 6 (1975) 35; 7 (1976) 304–305; 8 (1977) 369–370; 9 (1978) 416; 10 (1979) 278; 11 (1980) 43–49; 26 (1995) 336–337 | DES (1975) 21; (1993) 93; 27 (1996) 357.

Wandel: BRIT 2 (1971) 249; 18 (1987) 1–48 | GAJ 4 (1976) 6.

Midlothian

Elginhaugh: BRIT 3 (1972) 11; 12 (1981) 321; 14 (1983) 172–177 16 (1985) 264; 18 (1987) 312–313; 27 (1996) 357; 40 (2009) 365–368 | DES (1987) 31–32; (2007) 128–129.

Hanson, W. S., *A Roman Frontier Fort in Scotland: Elginhaugh* (Tempus: Stroud, 2007).

Hanson, W. S., *Elginhaugh: A Flavian Fort and Its Annexe* (Society for the Promotion of Roman Studies: London, 2007).

Carlops Spittal: BRIT 17 (1986) 371; 18 (1987) 32–33 | RCS 113.

Woodhead: BRIT 14 (1983) 167–181.

Moray

Auchinhove: DES (1974) 5 | JRS 41 (1951) 65; 48 (1958) 93; 51 (1961) 123.

Bellie: BRIT 17 (1986) 370 DES (1984) 12 | JRS 59 (1969) 113–114 | RCS 324-325 | TRS 122-125.

The Chevalier de Johnstone, *A Memoir of the Forty-Five* (London: Folio Society, 1958).

Muiryfold: JRS 51 (1961) 123; 59 (1969) 118.

Perth and Kinross

Abernethy (Carey): AJ 111 (1954) 26–105 | BRIT 26 (1995) 60 | JRS 63 (1973) 219 | PSAS 33 (1899) 13–33.

Ardoch: AJ 121 (1964) 196 | BRIT 1 (1970) 163–171; 2 (1971) 248; 3 (1972) 5; 9 (1978) 410; 15 (1984) 217–221; 16 (1985) 326; 26 (1995) 344; 28 (1997) 405–406 | DES (1956) 6; (1973) 41; (1986) 40–41; (1993) 99; (1996) 81; (1997) 62; (1999) 70; (2002) 90–91; (2017) 139 | PSAS 32 (1898) 399–476; 102 (1970) 122–128; 123 (1993) 291–313.

Breeze, D. J., 'The Roman Forts at Ardoch' in: O'Connor, A., Clarke, D. V. (eds.), *From the Stone Age to the "Forty-Five": Studies Presented to R B K Stevenson, Former Keeper, National Museum of Antiquities of Scotland* (John Donald Publishers, 1983), pp. 224–236.

Bertha: BRIT 3 (1972) 5; 5 (1974) 402; 40 (2009) 226–227 DES (1958) 30; (1999) 73; (2008) 155 | JRS 49 (1959) 136–137 | OSA XV 528 | PSAS 116 (1986) 197 | TRS 61.

Cargill: BRIT 13 (1982) 335–336; 18 (1987) 16 | DES (1981) 88; (2005) 104; (2006) 129; (1965) 30; (2003) 104 | JRS 33 (1943) 47; 48 (1958) 91; 56 (1966) 198 | RFF 151.

Dalginross: BRIT 39 (208) 274 | DES (1990) 44; (1992) 79; (1999) 70; (2006) 131 | GAJ 4 (1976) 25 | JRS 51 (1962) 162; 55 (1965) 81; 59 (1969) 109 PSAS 139 (2009) 273–274 | RFF 49–50.

Dunning: BRIT 20 (1989) 269–270; 26 (1995) 51–62 | DES (1974) 52; (1988) 27; (1993) 27, 102; (1998) 376; (2009) 149; (2013) 151–152; (2014) 162–163 | JRS 63 (1973) 218–219.

Fendoch: DES (1984) 43; (2004) 105–106 | JRS 28 (1938) 169 | PSAS 70 (1935) 110–154; 73 (1939) 110–154.

Gask Ridge Towers: See individual entries in *Rome's First Frontier, Beyond the Empire: A Guide to the Roman Remains in Scotland, Proceedings of the Society of Antiquaries of Scotland*, and www.canmore.org.uk.

Glenbank: BRIT 18 (1987) 16–17 | DES (1984) 4; (1998) 73; (1999) 70 PSAS 139 (2009) 273–274.

Gourdie, Steed Stalls: BRIT 18 (1987) 27 | DES (1959) 27 | JRS 33 (1943) 47–49; 41 (1951) 64 | PSAS 36 (1902) 182–203.

Inchtuthil: AC 37 | BRIT 18 (1987) 27 | DES (1952) 10–11; (1955) 21; (1956) 19; (1957) 23; (1958) 29–30; (1959) 27–28; (2009) 145; (2010) 136–137; (2011) 46 | JRS 43 (1953) 104; 44 (1954) 84; 45 (1955) 122–123; 46 (1956) 122; 47 (1956) 198–199; 48 (1958) 91; 49 (1959) 103–104; 50 (1959) 213; 51 (1961) 123, 160; 55 (1965) 82–83 | PSAS 36 (1901) 182–242; 121 (1991) 27–44.

Pitts, L. F., St Joseph, J. K., *Inchtuthil: The Roman Legionary Fortress* (Society for the Promotion of Roman Studies: London, 1985).

Kaims Castle: AJ 121 (1964) 196 | GAJ 4 (1976) 22 | PSAS 35 (1900) 18–21.

Strageath: BRIT 2 (1971) 248; 5 (1974) 402; 6 (1975) 225–226; 7 (1976) 300; 8 (1978) 361–363; 9 (1978) 410; 11 (1980) 351–352; 12 (1981) 319; 13 (1982) 336–337; 14 (1983) 284–287; 15 (1984) 275–276; 16 (1985) 263–264; 17 (1986) 371; 18 (1987) 309–310; 39 (2007) 274; 40 (2008) 227 | JRS 41 (1951) 63; 48 (1958) 90 | RFF 112.

Frere, S. S., Wilkes, J. J., *Strageath: Excavations Within the Roman Fort 1973–1986* (Society for the Promotion of Roman Studies: London, 1989).

Renfrewshire

Barochan Hill: BRIT 4 (1973) 275; 16 (1985) 265–267; 17 (1986) 311–313 | DES (1972) 49; (1979) 40; (1984) 34; (1985) 49; (1986) 39; (1993) 91 | GAJ 16 (1996) 41–76.

Scottish Borders

Cappuck: DES (1949) 11; (1974) 61 | GAJ 4 (1976) 6 | PSAS 46 (1911) 446–483; 85 (1951) 138–145.
Laidlaw, W., *On the remains of the Roman station at Cappuck, Roxburgh. History of the Berwickshire Naturalists Club*, 14 (1894), pp. 382–389.
Castlecraig: JRS 59 (1969) 104–128.
Easter Happrew: BRIT 28 (1997) 412 DES (1955) 21; (1999) 79–80 | PSAS 90 (1957) 93–101.
Eshiels: JRS 55 (1965) 78–79.
Newstead: BRIT 3 (1972) 8–9; 19 (1988) 431; 22 (1991) 232; 25 (1994) 261; 26 (1995) 339–341; 28 (1997) 412; 29 (1998) 381; 33 (2002) 290 | DES (1991) 7; (1992) 7; (1993) 7; (1994) 5; (1996) 89–90; (2005) 125 | JRS 39 (1949) 99; 48 (1958) 87–88 | PSAS 1 (1851) 28–33; 58 (1923) 309–324; 84 (1949) 1–38; 121 (1991) 215–222; 129 (1999) 373–391; 130 (2000) 457–467.
Curle, J. (ed.), *A Roman Frontier Post and Its People: The Fort of Newstead in the Parish of Melrose* (Glasgow: James Maclehose and Sons, 1911).
Hunter, F. & Keppie, L. J. F. (eds.), *A Roman Frontier Post and its People: Newstead 1911–2011* (Edinburgh: NMSE Publishing, 2015).
Oakwood: BRIT 3 (1972) 10 | DES (1949) 11 | PSAS 80 (1945) 103–117; 86 (1952) 202–205.

Stirling

Bochastle: DES (1948) 9–10; (1949) 10; (1953) 13–14; (1974) 52; (1998) 93; (2006) 164–165 | JRS 59 (1969) 109.
Anderson, W. A., Taylor, C. & Sommerville, A., 'The Roman fort at Bochastle, by Callander', *Transactions of the Glasgow Archaeological Society* (New Series), (1956), 14: 35–63.
Doune: BRIT 15 (1984) 217–223, 275; 16 (1985) 264; 18 (1987) 17; 31 (2000) 381; 40 (2009) 227 | DES (1984) 4; (1999) 87; (2010) 167 | RFF 84.

Drumquhassle: BRIT 9 (1978) 411; 10 (1979) 275; 14 (1983) 168–172; 29 (1998) 379; 31 (2000) 381 | DES (1978) 1; (2000) 89; (2004) 127–128 | SAJ 24(2) (2010) 147–168.

Hillside, Dunblane: BRIT 27 (1996) 398 | DES (1966) 37–38; (1967) 36; (1995) 14 | GAJ 1 (1969) 35–36 | JRS 41 (1951) 52-65; 59 (1969) 114.

Malling: BRIT 9 (1978) 41; 15 (1984) 275; 18 (1987) 29 | DES (1974) 52; (2011) 179–180 | JRS 59 (1969) 109–110; 63 (1973) 223–224.

West Lothian

Castle Greg: BRIT 20 (1989) 271; 41 (2010) 352 | DES (2012) 182–183; (2013) 188; (2015) 194.

Index of Roman Sites

Abernethy (Carey) (Camp), 7, 23, 61–62, 66, 91
Ardoch (Fort, Camps), 7, 22, 24, 62–63, 70, 78, 80, 91
Auchinhove (Camp), 7, 27, 58–59, 61, 91

Bankend (see Beattock and Dalswinton)
Bankfoot (see Dalswinton)
Barnhill (see Beattock)
Barochan Hill (Fort), 7, 70–71, 93
Beattock (Bankend, Barnhill) (Camp, Fortlet), 7, 37–38, 89
Bellie (Camps), 7, 59–60, 91
Bertha (Fort), 7, 20, 22, 63–64, 92
Birrens (Fort, Camp), 7, 37, 38–39, 46, 74, 89
Bochastle (Fort, Camp), 7, 20, 46, 74, 76, 77–78, 93
Broomholm (Fort), 7, 39, 89
Burnfield (Camp), 7, 26, 27–28, 58, 88

Camelon, North and South (Forts), 7, 48, 49–50, 90
Cappuck (Fort), 7, 72, 93
Cardean (Fort), 7, 32, 88
Carey (see Abernethy)
Cargill (Fort, Fortlet), 7, 20, 64, 92

Carlops Spittal (Camps), 7, 19, 52, 56–57, 91
Carnwath (Camp, Fortlet), 7, 50–51, 90
Castle Greg (Fortlet), 7, 20, 51, 83–84, 94
Castlecraig (Camp), 7, 73, 93
Castledykes (Fort, Camps), 7, 46, 51–52, 90
Cold Chapel (Camp), 7, 52, 90
Cornhill (Camp), 7, 52, 90
Crawford (Fort), 7, 20, 24, 40, 52–53, 90

Dalginross (Fort, Camp), 7, 20, 65, 79, 92
Dalswinton (Bankfoot, Bankend) (Forts, Camps), 7, 15, 20, 39–40, 89
Denholm (Eastcote) (Camp), 7, 40, 89
Doune (Fort), 7, 20, 78–79, 80, 93
Drumlanrig (inc. Islafoot) (Fort, Camp), 7, 40–41, 89
Drumquhassle (Fort), 7, 20
Dun (Camp), 7
Dunning (Camp), 7
Durisdeer (Camp), 7

Eastcote (see Denholm)
Easter Happrew (Fort), 7
Elginhaugh (Fort), 7
Eshiels (Camps), 7

Fendoch (Fort, Camp, Fortlet), 7
Fourmerkland (Camp), 7, 31, **79–80**, 94

Gask Ridge (Towers), 7, 17, 24, 62, 87
Gatehouse of Fleet (Fortlet), 7, 20, **43**, 90
Girvan Mains (Camps), 7, **35–36**, 89
Glenbank (Fortlet), 7, 20, 24, **67**, 69, 92
Glenlochar (Fort, Camp), 7, 20, **44–45**, 90
Glenluce (Camp), 7, 35, **45**, 90
Glenmailen (Ythan Wells) (Camps), 7, **27–28**, 88
Gogar Green (Camp), 7, **48**, 90
Gourdie, Steed Stalls (Camp), 7, **67–68**, 92

Hillside, Dunblane (Camps), 7, **80–81**, 94

Inchtuthil (Legionary Fortress, Camps), 7, 14, 64, 67, **68–69**, 85
Inverquharity (Fortlet, Camp), 7, 20, **33–34**, 89
Islafoot (see Drumlanrig)

Kaims Castle (Fortlet), 7, 9, 20, 24, **69–70**, 92
Kintore (Camp), 7, 15, **28–29**, 88
Kirkhouse (Camp), 7, **53–54**, 57, 91
Kirkland (Fortlet), 7, 20, **46**, 90

Lake of Menteith (see Malling)
Lamington (Camp), 7, **54**, 91

Lochlands (Camps), 7, 15, 49, **50**, 90
Logie Durno (Camp), 7, **29**, 88
Loudoun Hill (Fort), 7, 35, **36–37**, 40, 52, 89

Malling (Fort, Camps), 7, 20, **81–82**, 94
Milton (Fort, Camps), 7, 20, 37, **46**, 76, 90
Mollins (Fort), 7, **55**, 91
Muiryfold (Camp), 7, 27, 58, **60–61**, 91

Newstead (Forts, Camps), 7, 20, 45, 46, 74, **75–76**, 93
Normandykes (Camp), 7, 15, 29, **30**, 88

Oakwood (Fort, Camp), 7, 20, **76–77**, 93

Raeburnfoot (Camp), 7, **46–47**, 90
Raedykes (Camp), 7, 19, **31**, 88

Stracathro (Fort, Camp), 7, 16, 28, **34–35**, 40, 89
Strageath (Fort), 7, **70**, 92

Trimontium (see Newstead)

Wandel (Camp), 7, 52, **55**, 57, 91
Ward Law (Camp), 7, **47–48**, 90
Woodhead (Camp), 7, **57–58**, 91

Ythan Wells (see Glenmailen)